The Shop

Illustrations by Trevor Dunton

Robinson Children's Books

First published in the UK by Robinson Children's Books,
an imprint of Constable & Robinson Ltd, 2001

Robinson & Constable Ltd
3 The Lanchesters
162 Fulham Palace Road
London
W6 9ER

This collection © Constable & Robinson 2001
Illustrations © Trevor Dunton 2001

All rights reserved. This book is sold subject to the condition
that it shall not, by way of trade or otherwise, be lent,
re-sold, hired out or otherwise circulated in any form of
binding or cover other than that in which it is published and
without a similar condition including this condition being
imposed on the subsequent purchaser.

A copy of the British Library Cataloguing in Publication Data
for this title is available from the British Library

ISBN 1-84119-159-0

Printed and bound in the EC

10 9 8 7 6 5 4 3 2 1

To all our customers,

Welcome to the biggest and best joke shop in the world!

Whether you're looking for that special new baby joke, a smashing joke about china, a marvellous monster joke, or simply want to try on a hat or coat joke for size, you'll find it in our store.

Don't forget to check out our cut-price jokes and howlers in the bargain basement or, if money's no object, our truly priceless jokes in the jewellery department.

And if you need a spot of light refreshment or even a slap-up meal, why not try our self-service cafe or restaurant (where you'll find our waiters most attentive).

Other shop services include key-cutting, photo developing and banking — and we even have a doctor's surgery, opticians and travel agency . . . You'll find our full store directory on the next page.

Have fun and happy shopping!

Carrie R. Bag
Store Manager

Store Directory

GROUND FLOOR

FIRST FLOOR

SECOND FLOOR

THIRD FLOOR

FOURTH FLOOR

GROUND FLOOR

SERVICES
Meet the Staff

Laura: Whenever I go to the joke shop the sales assistant shakes my hand.
Lionel: I expect it's to make sure you don't put it in the till.

The new sales assistant came into the store manager's office and said, "I think you're wanted on the phone, sir."
"What d'you mean, you think?" demanded the manager.
"Well, sir, the phone rang, I answered it and a voice said, 'Is that you, you old fool?' "

"If you're going to work here, young man," said the
store manager, "one thing you must learn is that we
are very keen on cleanliness in this shop. Did you
wipe your feet on the mat as you came in?"
"Oh, yes, madam."
"And another thing, we are very keen on
truthfulness. There is no mat."

"I just want you to remember one thing, Boyce,"
said the store manager to the new shop assistant.
"If at first you don't succeed – you're fired!"

A sales assistant was being interviewed for a job
and asked the store manager what the hours were.
"We try to have early hours you know. I hope that
suits."
"Of course," said the sales assistant. "I don't mind
how early I leave."

"Good morning, sir. I'm applying for the job as the store handyman."
"I see. Well, are you handy?"
"Oh yes. I only live next door."

Did you hear about the headless horseman who got a job in a department store?
He's the head buyer.

Customer Information

When is a shop like a boat?
When it has sales.

Notice in a new shop window:
Don't go elsewhere and be robbed — try us!

Where do ghosts go shopping?
In boo-tiques.

First customer: My brother's just opened a store.
Second customer: Really? How's he doing?
First customer: Six months. He opened it with a crowbar.

What do you get if you cross an eel with a shopper?
A slippery customer.

Escalators

A man went into the local department store where he saw a sign on the escalator – Dogs must be carried on this escalator. The man then spent the next two hours looking for a dog.

Doctor! Doctor! My sister thinks she's an elevator.
Tell her to come in.
I can't. She doesn't stop at this floor.

Toilets
What do you call an American with a lavatory on his head?
John.

Banking and Money Exchange

Why is money called dough?
Because we all knead it.

What happened when the puss swallowed a nickel?
There was money in the kitty.

Where do bees keep their money?
In a honey-box.

Three animals were having a drink in a cafe, when the owner asked for the money. "I'm not paying," said the duck. "I've only got one bill and I'm not breaking it."

"I've spent my last buck," said the deer.

"Then the duck'll have to pay," said the skunk. "Getting here cost me my last scent."

Key-Cutting

"What is your occupation?" asked the judge.

"I'm a locksmith, your Honor."

"And what were you doing in the jeweller's shop at three in the morning when the police officers entered?"

"Making a bolt for the door!"

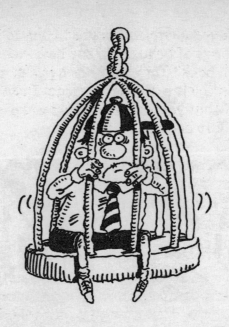

What if you can't work the lock on your door?
Sing until you get the right key.

Please sir! Please sir! Why do you keep me locked up
in this cage?
Because you're the teacher's pet.

Why don't you get locks on cemetery gates?
There's no point — all the ghosts have skeleton keys.

Photo Developing

What do you think of this photograph of me?
It makes you look older, frankly.
Oh, well, it'll save the cost of having another one
taken later on.

One day Tony's girlfriend wrote to him to say their friendship was off and could she have her photograph back? Tony sent her a pile of pictures of different girls with the message: I can't remember what you look like. Could you please take out your photo and return the rest.

Poor old Stephen sent his photograph off to a Lonely Hearts Club. They sent it back saying that they weren't that lonely.

Wedding List

At a very classy wedding, one of the guests broke wind. The bridegroom was furious and rounded on the guilty party. "How dare you break wind in front of my wife?" he roared.
"Sorry," said the guest. "Was it her turn?"

What happened at the cannibal's wedding party? They toasted the bride and groom.

Car Parking

A man was in court charged with parking his car in a restricted area. The judge asked if he had anything to say in his defense. "They shouldn't put up such misleading notices," said the man. "It said FINE FOR PARKING HERE."

What do you get if you cross a Rolls-Royce with a vampire?
A monster that attacks expensive cars and sucks out their gas tanks.

What purrs along the road and leaves holes in the lawn?
A Moles-Royce.

What kind of snake is useful on your windscreen?
A viper.

Two wizards in a car were driving along and the police were chasing them for speeding. One said, "What are we going to do?"
The other replied, "Quick, turn the car into a side street."

What happens when a frog's car breaks down?
It gets toad away.

Why did the car judder to a stop when it saw a ghost?
It had a nervous breakdown.

If you watch the way that many motorists drive you will soon reach the conclusion that the most dangerous part of a car is the nut behind the wheel.

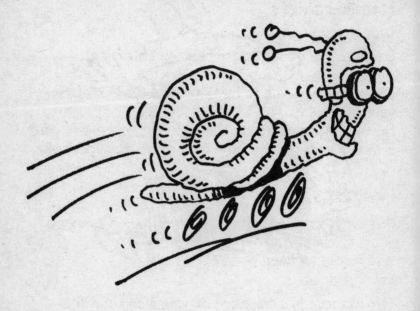

What sort of a car has your dad got?
I can't remember the name. I think it starts with T.
Really? Ours only starts with petrol.

What petrol do snails prefer?
Shell.

How do you stop a werewolf howling in the back of a car?
Put him in the front.

ACCESSORIES

Handkerchiefs

Why did the viper viper nose?
Because the adder adder handkerchief.

Simon: I was going to buy you a handkerchief for
your birthday.
Sarah: That was a kind thought. But why didn't you?
Simon: I couldn't find one big enough for your nose.

Handbags

Did you hear about the monster who had an extra
pair of hands?
Where did he keep them?
In a handbag.

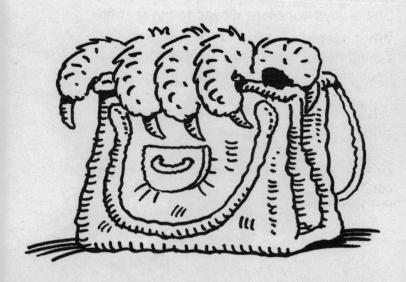

Where does a witch keep her purse?
In a hag bag.

Why are glow-worms good to carry in your bag?
They can lighten your load.

Gloves

Two people went into a very dark, spooky cave. "I can't see a thing," said one.
"Hold my hand," said the other.
"All right." The first man reached out. "Take off that horrible bristly glove first, though."
"But I'm not wearing a glove. . ."
What makes an ideal present for a monster?
Five pairs of gloves — one for each hand.

Did you hear about the witch who was ashamed of her long black hair?
She always wore long gloves to cover it up.

Sunglasses

What did
Tarzan say
when he saw
the monsters
coming?
Here come the
monsters.
And what did
he say when
he saw the
monsters
coming with
sunglasses on?
Nothing – he didn't recognize them!

Umbrellas

A family of tortoises went into a cafe for some ice-cream. They sat down and were about to start when Father Tortoise said, "I think it's going to rain. Junior, will you pop home and fetch my umbrella?"
So off went Junior for Father's umbrella, but three days later he still hadn't returned.
"I think, dear," said Mother Tortoise to Father Tortoise, "that we had better eat Junior's ice cream before it melts."
And a voice from the door said, "If you do that I won't go."

Did you hear about the sword swallower who swallowed an umbrella?
He wanted to put something away for a rainy day.

Hats

What happened to the witch with an upside-down nose?
Every time she sneezed her hat blew off.

First Woman: Whenever I'm down in the dumps I buy myself a new hat.
Second Woman: Oh, so that's where you get them.

While visiting close friends, a gnat,
Decided to sleep in a hat.
But an elderly guest
Decided to rest
Now the gnat and the hat are quite flat.

A police officer was escorting a prisoner to jail when his hat blew off. "Shall I run and get it for you?" asked the prisoner obligingly.
"You must think I'm daft," said the officer. "You stand here and I'll get it."

Watches

Doctor: You seem to be in excellent health, Mrs Brown. Your pulse is as steady and regular as clockwork.
Mrs Brown: That's because you've got your hand on my watch.

"I hope you're not one of those boys who sits and watches the school clock," said the principal to a new boy.
"No, sir. I've got a digital watch that bleeps at half past three."

PERFUME AND COSMETICS

Perfume, Aftershave and Soap

What perfume do lady snakes like to wear?
"Poison" by Dior.

What happened when the monster stole a bottle of perfume?
He was convicted of fragrancy.

"What's your new perfume called?" a young man asked his girlfriend.
"High Heaven," she replied.
"I asked what it was called, not what it smells like!"

Jerry: Is that a new perfume I smell?
Kerry: It is, and you do!

Jane: Have you noticed that your mother smells a bit funny these days?
Wayne: No. Why?
Jane: Well, your sister told me she was giving her a bottle of toilet water for her birthday.

What aftershave do monsters wear?
Brute.

Why did the sailor grab a bar of soap when his ship sank?
He thought he could wash himself ashore.

Cosmetics

Susannah was watching her big sister covering her face with cream. "What's that for?" she asked.
"To make me beautiful," came the reply. Susannah then watched in silence as her sister wiped her face clean.
"Doesn't work, does it?" she said.

Gill: Your sister uses too much make-up.
Jen: Do you think so?
Gill: Yes. It's so thick that if you tell her a joke, five minutes after she's stopped laughing her face is still smiling!

19

Nail Polish

How do snails get their shells all shiny?
They use snail polish.

JEWELLERY

A jeweler standing behind the counter of his shop was astounded to see a man come hurtling head-first through the window. "What on earth are you up to?" he demanded.
"I'm terribly sorry," said the man, "I forgot to let go of the brick!"

Diamonds

A little thing, a pretty thing, without a top or bottom. What am I?
A diamond ring.

What's the best place to find diamonds?
In a pack of cards.

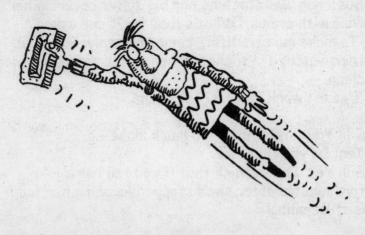

TRULY PRICELESS

What's thick, black, floats on water and shouts
"Knickers!"?
Crude oil.
What is black, gushes out of the ground and shouts
"Excuse me"?
Refined oil.

The box-office clerk at the theater went to the
manager's office to tell him that there were two
horses in the foyer. "Two horses?" exclaimed the
manager in surprise. "What on earth do they want?"
"Two stalls for Monday night."

What do you call a neurotic octopus?
A crazy, mixed-up squid.

How did the baker get an electric shock?
He stood on a bun and a current ran up his leg.

Where do you find giant snails?
On the end of a giant's fingers.

Who has large antlers, has a high voice and wears white gloves?
Mickey Moose.

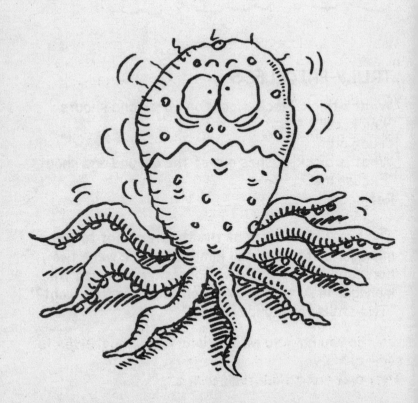

What's the difference between a sigh, a car and a monkey?
A sigh is oh, dear. A car is too dear. A monkey is you, dear.

What kind of monster can sit on the end of your finger?
The bogeyman.

What do you call a rich frog?
A gold-blooded reptile.

Two weevils came to town from the country. One worked hard and became very rich. The other became the lesser of two weevils.

Why do you have to wait so long for a ghost train to come along?
They only run a skeleton service.

What do you get if you cross a mosquito with a knight?
A bite in shining armor.

What do you get if you cross an orange with a comedian?
Peels of laughter.

FIRST

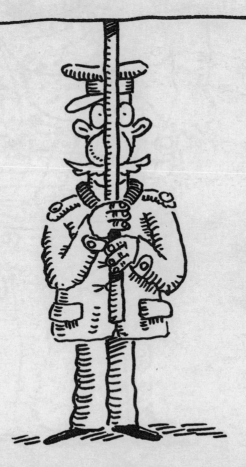

CLOTHES
Men's Clothes

Neckties
Waiter, waiter, your necktie is in my soup! That's all right, sir. It won't shrink.

What did the necktie say to the hat? You go on ahead and I'll hang around.

Underwear
What did the police officer say to his stomach? I've got you under a vest.

Mickey: Do have holes in your underpants?
Nicky: No, of course not.
Mickey: Then how do you get your feet through?

Socks
You've got your socks on inside out.
I know, Mom, but there are holes on the other side.

Jackets and Trousers
How do stones stop moths eating your jackets?
Because a rolling stone gathers no moths.

Why did the golfer wear an extra pair of trousers?
In case he got a hole in one.

Jumpers
What do you get if you cross a kangaroo with a sheep?
A woolly jumper.

Made to Measure
An extremely tall man with round shoulders, very long arms and one leg six inches shorter than the other went into a tailor's shop. "I'd like to see a suit that will fit me," he told the tailor.
"So would I, sir," the tailor sympathized. "So would I."

Who makes suits and eats spinach?
Popeye the Tailorman.

Evening Dress
What do you get if you cross a giant, hairy monster with a penguin?
I don't know but it's a very tight-fitting tuxedo.

At a very exclusive boarding school, one of the teachers who was going out for a grand dinner appeared wearing a tuxedo, evening shirt and black tie. "Oh, sir," said one of the boys. "You're not wearing those clothes are you? You know they always give you a headache in the morning."

Did you hear about the skeleton who wore a kilt?
He was called Boney Prince Charlie.

Ladies Clothes

Lingerie
Sports coach: Come on, Sophie. You can run faster than that.
Sophie: I can't, sir. I'm wearing run-resistant panty-hose.

Witch: Doctor, doctor, each time I put my bra on I get thunder and lightning on my stomach.
Doctor: That's all right, it's just a storm in a C-cup.

What's worse than ants in your pants?
A bat in your bra.

Dresses
What do you get if you cross a fashion designer with a sea monster?
The Loch Dress Monster.

Mommy monster: Did you catch everyone's eyes in that dress, dear?
Girl monster: Yes, mom, and I've brought them all home for Cedric to play marbles with.

Knock, knock.
Who's there?
Maggot.
Maggot who?
Maggot me this new dress today.

Why did the girl keep her dresses in the fridge?
She liked to have something cool to slip into in the
evening.

Did you hear about the lady ghoul who went to buy a
dress in the Phantom Fashion boutique? "I'd like to
try on that shroud in the window," she told the
ghoul in charge.
"Yes, ma'am," said the ghoul, "but wouldn't you
prefer to use the changing room instead?"

Yes, I do like your dress – but isn't it a little early
for Halloween?

Coats
English Teacher: Now give me a sentence using the
word "fascinate."
Clara: My raincoat has ten buttons but I can only
fasten eight.

What coat has the most sleeves?
A coat of arms.

Where do frogs keep their coats?
In the croakroom.

Lady: I'd like a fur coat, please.
Store assistant: Certainly, madam, what fur?
Lady: To keep myself warm, of course.

Why do bears wear fur coats?
They'd look silly in yellow raincoats.

Boy: Did you know you can get fur from a three-headed mountain monster?
Girl: Really? What kind of fur?
Boy: As fur away as possible!

What likes to spend the summer in a fur coat and the winter in a swimsuit?
A moth.

Flash Harry gave his girlfriend a mink stole for her birthday. Well, it may not have been mink, but it's fairly certain it was stole.

Party Wear

What should you do if you find yourself surrounded by Dracula, Frankenstein, a zombie and a werewolf? Hope you're at a fancy dress party.

What do you call a snake that is trying to become a bird?
A feather boa.

Tom: Did you got to Ann's party?
Max: No, the invitation said "from five to nine," and I'm ten.

Footwear

Boots

Why did the cowboy die with his boots on?
'Cos he didn't want to stub his toes when he kicked the bucket.

How do ghosts keep their feet dry?
By wearing boots.

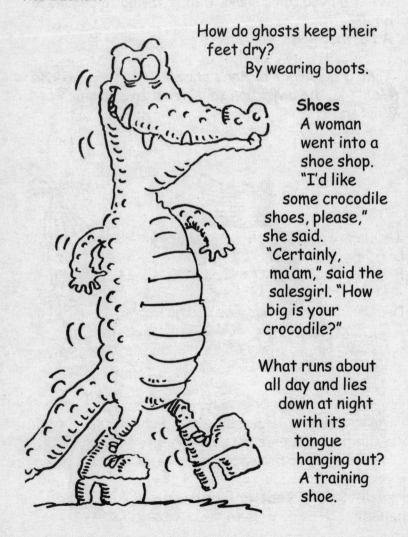

Shoes

A woman went into a shoe shop. "I'd like some crocodile shoes, please," she said. "Certainly, ma'am," said the salesgirl. "How big is your crocodile?"

What runs about all day and lies down at night with its tongue hanging out?
A training shoe.

Teacher: Fred! Wipe that mud off your shoes
before you come in the classroom.
Fred: But, sir, I'm not wearing any shoes.

Dad, would you like to save some money?
I certainly would, son. Any suggestions?
Sure. Why not buy me a bike, then I won't wear my
shoes out so fast.

Psychiatrist: Well, what's your problem?
Patient: I prefer brown shoes to black shoes.
Psychiatrist: There's nothing wrong with that. Lots
of people prefer brown shoes to black shoes. I do
myself.
Patient: Really? How do your like yours — fried or
boiled?

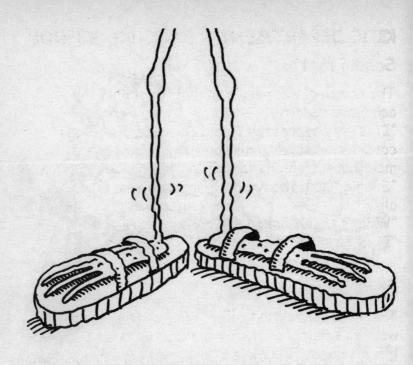

We're so poor that Mom and Dad can't afford to buy me shoes. I have to polish my feet and lace my toes together.

Sandals
What kind of shoes do frogs like?
Open-toad sandals.

Slippers
A doctor visited his patient in the hospital ward after the operation. "I've got some bad news — we amputated the wrong leg. Now the good news — the man in the next bed wants to buy your slippers."

KIDS DEPARTMENT – BACK TO SCHOOL

School Motto

The principal was very proud of his school's academic record.

"It is very impressive," said one parent who was considering sending his son there. "How do you maintain such high standards?"

"Simple," said the head. "The school motto says it all."

"What's that?" asked the parent.

"If at first you don't succeed, you're expelled."

First Day at School

There was once a lad called Willy Maufe. When he went to school for the first time the teacher asked him his name. "I'm Maufe," said Willy.

"Don't be silly, boy," said the teacher. "You'll stay here till 3.30 like the rest of us."

Mother: How was your first day at school?
Little Boy: OK, but I haven't got my present yet.
Mother: What do you mean?
Little Boy: Well, the teacher gave me a chair, and said, "Sit there for the present."

Teachers

Did you hear about the math teacher who fainted in class?
Everyone tried to bring her 2.

The math teacher and the English teacher went out for a quick pizza after school. "How long will the pizzas be?" asked the math teacher.
"Sorry, sir," replied the waiter, "we don't do long pizzas, just ordinary round ones."
Why was the cannibal expelled from school?
Because he kept buttering up the teacher.

"Well, children," said the cannibal cooking teacher.
"What did you make of the new English teacher?"
"Burgers, ma'am."

"Don't worry Miss Jones," said the principal to the new teacher. "You'll cope with your new class, but they'll keep you on your toes."
"How's that, sir?" asked the teacher.
"They always put drawing pins on the chairs."

The ghost teacher was giving her pupils instructions on how to haunt a house properly. "Has everyone got the hang of walking through walls?" she asked. One little ghoul at the front of the class looked uncertain. "Just watch the blackboard everyone," instructed the teacher, "and I'll go through it one more time."

English

What subject do young witches like best?
Spelling.

Teacher: Colin, one of your essays is very good but the other one I can't read.
Colin: Yes, sir. My mother is a much better writer than my father.

The class was set an essay on Shakespeare. Jacqui wrote in her book: Shakespeare wrote tragedy, comedy, and errors.

Math

Teacher: Are you good at arithmetic?
Mary: Well, yes and no.
Teacher: What do you mean, yes and no?
Mary: Yes, I'm no good at arithmetic.

Tom: Why are you scratching your head?
Harry: I've got those arithmetic bugs again.
Tom: Arithmetic bugs – what are they?
Harry: Well, some people call them head lice.
Tom: Then why do you call them arithmetic bugs?
Harry: Because they add to my misery, subtract from my pleasure, divide my attention and multiply like crazy!

Mary arrived home from school covered in spots.
"Whatever's the matter?" asked her mother.
"I don't know," replied Mary, "but the teacher thinks I may have caught decimals."

Teacher: I told you to write this poem out twenty times because your handwriting is so bad.
Girl: I'm sorry Miss – my math is not that good either.

What did the math book say to the geometry book?
Boy! Do we have our problems!

Teacher: What's the best way to pass this
geometry test?
Boy: Knowing all the angles?

History

Jennifer: How come you did so badly in history? I
thought you had all the dates written on your
sleeve?
Miriam: That's the trouble, I put on my geography
blouse by mistake.

What school subject are snakes best at?
Hiss-tory.

Geography

"Ann," said the teacher, "point out Australia for me on the map."
Ann went to the front of the class, picked up the pointer and showed the rest of the class where Australia was.
"Well done! Now, Alec! Can you tell us who discovered Australia?"
"Er . . . Ann, sir?"

Did you hear about the brilliant geography teacher?
He had abroad knowledge of his subject.
"Alec," groaned his father when he saw his son's school report. "Why are you so awful at geography?"
"It's the teacher's fault, Dad. He keeps telling us about places I've never heard of."

Homework

What do young ghosts write their homework in?
Exorcise books.

Teacher: Andrew, your homework looks as if it is in your father's handwriting.
Andrew: Well, I used his pen, sir.

Father: Would you like me to help you with your homework?
Son: No, thanks, I'd rather get it wrong by myself.

When is a blue school book not a blue school book?
When it is read.

Exams

Knock, knock.
Who's there?
Sacha.
Sacha who?
Sacha lot of questions in this exam!

Mother: Did you get a good place in the geography test?
Daughter: Yes, Mum, I sat next to the cleverest kid in the class.

How did dinosaurs pass exams?
With extinction.

Why did the flea fail his exams?
He wasn't up to scratch.

Girl: Mum, you know you're always worried about me failing my exam?
Mother: Yes.
Girl: Well, your worries are over.

Student: Excuse me, sir, but I don't think I deserve a mark of 0 for this exam paper.
Teacher: Neither do I, but it's the lowest mark I can give.

Which animals do you have to beware of when you take exams?
Cheetahs.

Boy: My sister's the school swot.
Girl: Does she do well in exams?
Boy: No, but she kills a lot of flies.

BABY DEPARTMENT

New Babies

Definition of a baby: A soft pink thing that makes a lot of noise at one end and has no sense of responsibility at the other.

What would you get if you crossed a new-born snake with a basketball?
A bouncing baby boa.

What are baby witches called?
Halloweenies.

What is a baby bee?
A little humbug.

Why did you drop the baby?
Well, Mrs Smith said he was a bonny bouncing baby, so I wanted to see if he did.

Did you hear about Mrs Dimwit's new baby? She thought babies should be pink, so she took this one to the doctor because it was a horrible yeller.

Baby Clothes and Nappies

Knock, knock.
Who's there?
Underwear.
Underwear who?
Underwear my baby is tonight?

Why are babies always gurgling with joy?
Because it's a nappy time.

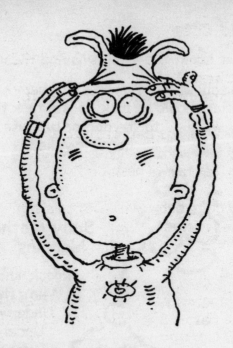

It can't go on! It can't go on!
What can't go on?
This baby's vest — it's too small for me.

Rattles and Dummies

How can you tell if a snake is a baby snake?
It has a rattle.

What do baby pythons play with?
Rattle-snakes.

What did the Pharaohs use to keep their babies
quiet?
Egyptian dummies.

Prams and Cots

Did you hear about the witch who had the ugliest baby in the world?
She didn't push the pram — she pulled it.

Mrs Brown: Who was that at the door?
Veronica: A lady with a baby in a buggy.
Mrs Brown: Tell her to push off.

How do you get a baby astronaut to sleep?
Get a cot and rock-et.

Baby Food

Doctor, doctor, my baby's swallowed a watch!
Give it some Epsom Salts: that should help it pass the time.

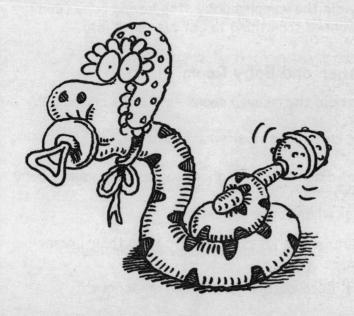

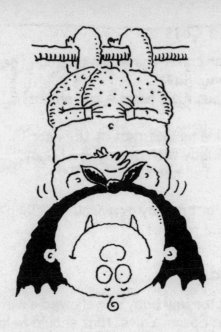

Why did the vampire baby stop having baby food?
He wanted something to get his teeth into.

Mother and Baby Room

What did the mommy snake say to the crying baby snake?
Stop crying and viper your nose.

What did the mother ghost say to the naughty baby ghost?
Spook when you're spooken to.

Baby snake to its mother: Are we poisonous?
Mother: Why?
Baby: Because I've just bitten my tongue!

GENERAL HOUSEHOLD

China

What kind of plate does a skeleton eat off?
Bone china.

Mom, you know that vase that's been handed down
from generation to generation?
Yes.
Well, this generation's dropped it.

Helen: Grandma, do you know what I'm going to give
you for your birthday?
Grandma: No, dear, what?
Helen: A nice teapot.
Grandma: But I've got a nice teapot.
Helen: No you haven't. I've just dropped it!

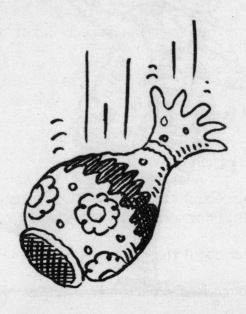

What did the bull say when he came out of the china shop?
I've had a smashing time.

Mirrors

What does a vampire say to the mirror?
Terror, terror on the wall.

Did you hear about the witch who was so ugly she kept sending her mirror back for repairs?

Did you hear about the witch who looked in the mirror?
It was a shattering experience.

Do you look in the mirror after you've washed?
No, I look in the towel!

Husband: Why have you put a mirror on the television set, dear?
Wife: Because I wanted to see what my family looks like.

Paintings and Prints

What did the picture say to the wall?
I've got you covered.

What's a ghost's favorite work of art?
A ghoulage.

Who is a bee's favorite painter?
Pablo Beecasso.

A very posh lady was walking around looking at the pictures in a department store when she stopped by one particular print. "I suppose this picture of a hideous witch is what you would call modern art?" she asked very pompously.

"No, ma'am," replied the assistant, "it's what we call a mirror."

Why are vampires artistic?
They're good at drawing blood.

Clocks

What happened when the werewolf swallowed a clock?
He got ticks.

((TICK))

((TOCK))

Teacher: Why are you always late?
Roger: I threw away my alarm clock.
Teacher: But why did you throw away your alarm clock?
Roger: Because it always went off when I was asleep.

You're late for work again, Lamport!
Yes, I'm sorry, sir. I overslept.
I thought I told you to get an alarm clock.
I did, sir, but there are nine of us in our family.
What's that got to do with it?
The alarm was only set for eight!

Hickory dickory dock
The mice ran up the clock.
The clock struck one,
And the rest got away with minor injuries.

You are so ugly your face would stop a clock.
And yours would make one run.

The proud owner of an impressive new clock was showing it off to a friend. "This clock," he said, "will go for fourteen days without winding."
"Really," replied his friend. "And how long will it go if you do wind it?"

Candles

Witch: How much are your black candles?
Salesman: Five pounds each.
Witch: That's candleous!

First witch: Shall I buy black or blue candles?
Second witch: Which one burns longer?
First witch: Neither, they both burn shorter.

Why did the mouse eat a
candle?
For light refreshment.

What's a cold, evil
candle called?
The wicked wick of
the north.

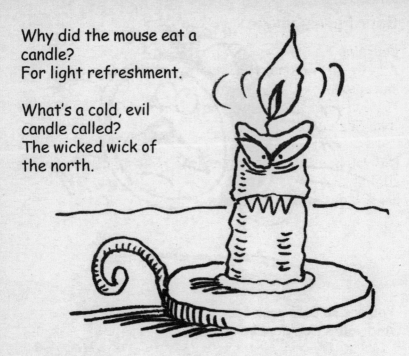

Lighting

A pretentious woman was showing a friend round
her new home. "It's very lovely," her friend
admitted, "but what you need in this big room is a
chandelier."
"I know, my dear," said her gracious hostess, "but
nobody in the family plays one."

Why did the teacher fix her bed to the chandelier?
Because she was a light sleeper.

Why did the monster eat a light bulb?
Because he was in need of light refreshment.

Soft Furnishings

Curtains
A little girl was next in line. "My name's Curtain," she said.
"I hope your first name's not Annette?"
"No. It's Velvet."

Did you hear about the man who tried to iron his curtains?
He fell out of the window.

Carpets and Rugs

Why did the moth nibble a hole in the carpet?
He wanted to see the floor show.
What do you call a wizard who lies on the floor?
Matt.

The wizard who had invented a flying carpet was
interviewed for a local radio station. "What's it like,
Merlin, to fly on a magic carpet?" asked the radio
presenter.
"Rugged," replied Merlin.

What's the definition of a nervous breakdown?
A chameleon on a tartan rug.

'Spose you think that's funny

Bedding and Towels
What do you get if you cross a sheep and a rainstorm?
A wet blanket.

What do snakes have on their bath towels?
Hiss and Hers.

Pattie: We had a burglary last night, and they took everything except the soap and towels.
Peter: The dirty crooks.

FURNITURE

Where did the witch get her furniture?
From the Ideal Gnome Exhibition.

Chairs and Sofas

How does Frankenstein sit in his chair?
Bolt upright.

What did the woodworm say to the chair?
It's been nice gnawing you!

Why did the principal put wheels on her rocking chair?
She liked to rock and roll.

Why did the termite eat a sofa and two chairs?
It had a suite tooth.

Tables

What's the longest piece of furniture in the school?
The multiplication table.

A stupid man was struggling out of his house with a
big table. His neighbor said to him, "Hello, Harry.
Where are you going with that then?"
And Harry replied, "I'm taking it to the store to
have it measured for a new tablecloth."

Beds

How can you tell if an elephant has been sleeping in your bed?
The sheets are wrinkled and the bed smells of peanuts.

Who stole the sheets from the bed?
Bed buglars.

Why did the composer spend all his time in bed?
He wrote sheet music.

What should you do if you find a snake in your bed?
Sleep in the wardrobe.

What do you call a python with a great bedside manner?
A snake charmer.

What should you do if you find a witch in your bed?
Run!

A cannibal known as Ned
Ate potato chips in his bed.
His mother said, Sonny
It's not very funny
Why don't you eat people instead?

Father: Why did you put a toad in your sister's bed?
Son: I couldn't find a spider.

Two friends who lived in the town were chatting.
"I've just bought a pig," said the first.
"But where will you keep it?" said the second. "Your yard's much too small for a pig!"
"I'm going to keep it under my bed," replied his friend.
"But what about the smell?"
"He'll soon get used to that."

When Mr Maxwell's wife left him, he couldn't sleep.
Why was that?
She had taken the bed.

I don't think my Mom knows much about children.
Why do you say that?
Because she always puts me to bed when I'm wide
awake, and gets me up when I'm sleepy!

I was once in a play called *Breakfast In Bed*.
Did you have a big role?
No, just toast and marmalade.

HARDWARE

Tools

How do you get a ghost to lie perfectly flat?
You use a spirit level.

No, Billy, you can't play with the hammer. You'll hurt your fingers.
No, I won't, Dad. Sis is going to hold the nails for me.

What's the safest way to use a hammer?
Get someone else to hold the nails.

An apprentice blacksmith was told by his boss to make a hammer. The lad had not the slightest idea how to begin, so he thought he'd be crafty and nip out and buy one. He duly showed the new hammer to his boss, who said, "That's excellent boy! Now make fifty more just like it!"

Mummy monster: What are you doing with that saw and where's your little brother?
Young monster: Hee, hee, he's my half-brother now.

Nails and Screws

What's the difference between a nail and a boxer?
One gets knocked in, the other gets knocked out.

Why did the man go out and buy a set of tools?
Because everyone kept telling him he had a screw loose.

Paint and Varnish

What is the best way to get paint off a chair?
Sit on it before the paint's dry.

Did you hear what daft Donald did when he offered to paint the garage for his dad in the summer holidays?
The instructions said put on three coats, so he went in and put on his blazer, his raincoat and his parka.

Jill: How awful that your aunt drowned in a tub of varnish.
Jack: Yes, but what a finish.

Tiles

What kind of tiles can't you stick on the wall?
Rep-tiles.

Putty

What happened to the man who couldn't tell the difference between porridge and putty?
All his windows fell out.

Ladders

Sign outside the school caretaker's hut:

WILL THE PERSON WHO BORROWED THE LADDER FROM THE CARETAKER PLEASE RETURN IT IMMEDIATELY OR FURTHER STEPS WILL BE TAKEN.

Buckets

What happened when the monster fell down a well?
He kicked the bucket.

What's the difference between school lunches and
a bucket of fresh manure?
School lunches are usually cold.

Police officer: Why are you driving with a bucket of
water on the passenger seat?
Driver: So I can dip my headlights.

BATH SHOP

Baths

Two small-time thieves had been sent by the Big Boss to steal a van-load of goods from a bathroom suppliers. One stayed in the van as look-out and the other went into the storeroom. Fifteen minutes went by, then half an hour, then an hour — and no sign of him. The look-out finally grew impatient and went to look for his partner. Inside the store the two came face to face. "Where have you been?" demanded the worried look-out.

"The boss told me to take a bath, but I couldn't find the soap and a towel."

What's the difference between a Peeping Tom and someone who's just got out of the bath?
One is rude and nosy. The other is nude and rosy.

It's batty on the wing

How do vampire football players get the mud off?
They all get in the bat-tub.

Which villains steal soap from the bath?
Robber ducks.

Boy: Dad, Dad, there's a spider in the bath.
Dad: What's wrong with that? You've seen spiders before.
Boy: Yes, but this one is as big as an octopus and is using all the hot water!

Robot: I have to dry my feet carefully after a bath.
Monster: Why?
Robot: Otherwise I get rusty nails.

Dr Frankenstein: I've just invented something that everyone in the world will want! You know how you get a nasty ring around the bathtub every time you use it, and you have to clean the ring off?
Igor: Yes, I hate it.
Dr Frankenstein: Well, you need never have a bathtub ring again! I've invented the square tub . . .

Did you hear about the idiot who had a new bath put in? The plumber said, "Would you like a plug for it?" The idiot replied, "Oh, I didn't know it was electric."

Hotel guest: Can you give me a room and a bath, please?
Porter: I can give you a room, but you'll have to wash yourself.

Mom: Joe, time for your medicine.
Joe: I'll run the bath then.
Mom: Why?
Joe: Because on the bottle it says "to be taken in water."

Does your brother keep himself clean?
Oh, yes. He takes a bath every month whether he needs one or not.

Showers

When is the water in the shower room musical?
When it's piping hot.

"Eureka!" shouted the famous scientist when he made an important discovery.
"Sorry, Professor," said his assistant. "I didn't have time to shower this morning."

What does a vampire stand on after taking a shower?
A bat mat.

Why did the burglar take a shower?
He wanted to make a clean getaway.

THIRD

ELECTRICAL GOODS

Vacuum Cleaners

Did you hear about the ghost who enjoyed doing housework?
He used to go round with the oooo-ver.

Teacher: Barbara, name three collective nouns.
Barbara: The wastepaper basket, the rubbish bin and the vacuum cleaner.

Irons

Doctor: Now tell me, Granny Perkins, how you happened to burn both your ears.
Granny Perkins: I was doing the ironing when the telephone rang, and I picked up the iron and put that to my ear by mistake.
Doctor: But you burnt both your ears!
Granny Perkins: Yes, well as soon as I put the phone down it rang again!

Why are most monsters covered in wrinkles?
Have you ever tried to iron a monster?

Toasters

Did you hear about the granny who plugged her electric blanket into the toaster by mistake?
She spent the night popping out of bed.

What did the toaster say to the bread?
Pop up and see me some time.

Kettles

Girl: Shall I put the kettle on?
Boy: No, I think you look all right in the dress you're wearing.

Ovens and Fridges

Did you hear about the time Eddy's sister tried to make a birthday cake?
The candles melted in the oven.

What is white one minute and brown the next?
A rat in a microwave oven.

What is brown one minute and white the next?
A rat in a freezer.

Telephones

Teacher: Who was that on the phone, Samantha?
Samantha: No one important, Miss. Just some man who said it was long distance from Australia, so I told him I knew that already.

How does a skeleton call his friends?
On a telebone.

What do ghosts use to phone home?
A terror-phone.

Vampire: Doctor, doctor, I keep thinking I'm a telephone.
Doctor: Why's that?
Vampire: I keep getting calls in the night.

At three o'clock one morning a veterinary surgeon was woken from a deep sleep by the ringing of his telephone. He staggered downstairs and answered the phone. "I'm sorry if I woke you," said a voice at the other end of the line.
"That's all right," said the vet, "I had to get up to answer the telephone anyway."

TVs, DVD Players and Video Recorders

John kept pestering his parents to buy a DVD player but they said they couldn't afford one. So one day John came home clutching a package containing a brand-new DVD. "Wherever did you get the money to pay for that?" asked his father suspiciously.
"It's all right, Dad," replied John, "I traded the TV in for it."

What is the safest way to see a witch?
On television.

How did the ghost song-and-dance act make a living?
By appearing in television spooktaculars.

Doctor, I keep stealing things. What can I do?
Try to resist the temptation, but if you can't, get me a new video player.

Daughter: What's on television tonight, Mom?
Mother: Same as always — a vase of flowers and a bowl of fruit.

Why did the cyclops buy a very small TV?
Because he only had one eye.

Computers

Computer teacher: Bob! Your work has certainly improved. There are only ten mistakes here.
Bob: Oh good!
Teacher: Now let's look at the second line, shall we?

The pupils in the 12th grade, who had learned to use computers, were being interviewed by prospective employers. Lisa was asked her typing speed. "I'm not sure," she replied. "But I can delete at 2,000 words a minute."

Cameras

Doctor, doctor, I've just swallowed the film from
my camera.
Well, let's hope nothing develops.

Why did Mr and Mrs Werewolf call their son
Camera?
Because he was always snapping.

FILMS AND MUSIC

Horror Films

What do you think of Dracula films?
Fangtastic!

Science Fiction Films

What film do you get if you cross a galaxy with a toad?
Star Warts.

Which space movie stars Count Dracula?
The Vampire Strikes Back.

What did The Terminator say to Batman?
I'll be bat!

Romances

Romeo: You
remind me of a
film star.
Juliet: Which
one?
Romeo: Lassie.

Cowboy Films

What film do you get if you cross the Lone Ranger with an insect?
The Masked-quito.

What did the cowboy maggot
say when he went into the saloon bar?
Gimme a slug of whiskey.

Who is in cowboy films and is always broke?
Skint Eastwood.

Billy and Bobby were watching a John Wayne video on TV. In one scene John Wayne was riding madly towards a cliff. "I bet you this chocolate bar that he falls over that cliff," said Billy.
"Done," said Bobby. John Wayne rode straight over the cliff. As Mick handed over his chocolate bar, Billy said, "I feel a bit guilty about this, I've seen the film before."
"So have I," said Bobby, "but I didn't think he'd be fool enough to make the same mistake twice."

What do you call a frog who wants to be a cowboy?
Hoppalong Cassidy.

The swing doors of the Wild West saloon crashed open and in came Little Pete, black with fury. "All right!" he raged, "All right! Who did it? What goldarned varmint painted my horse blue?"
The huge figure of Black Jake, notorious gunfighter and town baddie rose from a chair by the door. "It

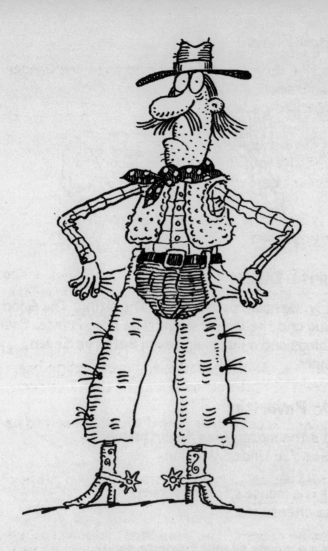

was me, shrimp," he drawled, bunching his gigantic fists, "what about it?"

"Oh, well, er," stammered little Pete wretchedly, "all I wanted to say was. . . when are you going to give it another coat?"

Favorite Insect Films

The Fly; Batman; Beetlejuice; The Sting; The Good, the Bug and the Ugly; Spawn; The Frog Prince; Four Webbings and a Funeral; Seven Bats for Seven Brothers.

Music Favorites

What's the mosquitoes' favorite song?
I've Got You Under My Skin.

What is a mouse's favorite song?
Please cheese me.

What's a mouse's least favorite song?
What's up Pussycat.

What song do snakes like to sing?
Viva Aspana.

What's a vampire's favorite love song?
How Can I Ignore the Girl Necks Door.

Did you hear about the musical ghost?
He wrote haunting melodies.

What song does a ghost sing to warn people that
he's around?
Beware My Ghoulish Heart.

Pop Groups

What do you call a top girl band made up of nits?
The Lice Girls.

What did the bat pop group call themselves?
The Boom Town Bats.

Which is the bees' favorite pop group?
The Bee Gees.

these Goulish things

Classical Music

What is a snake's favorite opera?
Wriggletto.

Why did the opera singer have such a high-pitched voice?
She had falsetto teeth.

When is an opera singer not an opera singer?
When he's a little hoarse.

Why did the music student have a piano in the bathroom?
Because he was practising Handel's Water Music.

BOOKS

Bookworms

Why did the sparrow fly into the bookstore?
It was looking for bookworms.

What would you do if you found a bookworm chewing your favorite book?
Take the words right out of its mouth.

What is a bookworm's idea of a big feast?
War and Peace.

Short Stories and Novels

Did you hear the story of the three holes?
Well, well, well.
What's a giant's favorite tale?
A tall story.

What do you call A Tale of Two Mosquitoes?
A bite-time story.

What is the bees' favorite novel?
The Great Gats-bee.

What's a man-eating monster's favorite novel?
Ghouliver's Travels.

So I said 'Who are you calling abominable?'

What is the Abominable Snowman's favorite novel?
War and Frozen Peas.

A frog walked into a bookstore and asked the owner
what he would recommend. "How about this sir?"
asked the bookstore owner, showing him *Toad of
Toad Hall*.
"Reddit, reddit," said the frog.

Ivan: What are you reading?
Andrea: It's a book about electricity.
Ivan: Oh, current events?
Andrea: No, light reading.

Reference

Crossword Fan: I've been trying to think of a word for two weeks!
Friend: How about a fortnight?

Bill: Do you like the dictionary I bought you for your birthday?
Ben: Sure. It's a great present but I just can't find the words to thank you enough.

Science Fiction

Teacher: I was going to read you a story called *The Invasion of the Body Snatchers*, but I've changed my mind.
Class: Oh why, ma'am?
Teacher: Because we might get carried away.

What's a flea's favorite science fiction book?
The Itch-hiker's Guide to the Galaxy.

Authors

Who wrote Count Dracula's life story?
The ghost writer.

What did the astronaut say to the author?
I took your book into orbit and I couldn't put it down.

Teacher: You seem to be exceedingly ignorant, Williams. Have you read Dickens?
Williams: No, sir.
Teacher: Have you read Shakespeare?
Williams: No, sir.
Teacher: Well, what have you read?
Williams: Er . . . er . . . I've red hair, sir.

Horror

The Bad-Tempered Werewolf — by Claudia Armoff
The Vampire's Victim — by E. Drew Blood
I Saw a Vampire — by Ron Fast
Escape From the Vampire — by Jess N. Time
Foaming at the Mouth — by Dee Monic
The Omen — by B. Warned
Don't Go Near Dracula — by Al Scream
The Witch Meets Dracula — by Pearce Nex

Ghost Stories

Black Magic – by Sue Pernatural
The Ghost of the Witch – by Eve L. Spirit
A Ghost in My House – by Olive N. Fear

Witchcraft

Never Make a Witch Angry – by Sheila Tack
Going on a Witch Hunt – by Count Miout
I Saw a Witch – by Denise R. Knockin
I Saw a Witch in the Mirror – by Douglas Cracked
When a Wizard Knocks on Your Door – by Wade Aminit
Wizard from Another Planet – by A. Lee-En

Hobbies

Bungee Jumping with Monsters — by Wade R. Go
Collecting Mosquitoes — by Ethan Alive
Collecting Reptiles — by Ivor Frog
Collecting Wriggly Creatures — by Tina Worms
Keeping Mosquitoes — by Lara Bites
Keeping Pet Snakes — by Sir Pent
Tracking Monsters — by Woody Hurt
How to Feed Dogs — by Nora Bone
Telling Fortunes with a Crystal Ball — by Thea Lot
When to go Monster-Hunting — by Mae B. Tomorrow
Cooking with Pork — by Chris P. Bacon

Biography and Autobiography

Me and the Wife — by Ian Shee
My Best Friend, the Witch — by Ann Otherwitch
I Met an Abominable Snowman — by Anne Tarctic
I Caught the Loch Ness Monster — by Janet A. Big-Wun

Self-Help

How to Escape from a Witch — by Shelby Lucky
How to Keep Vampires From Your House — by Dora Steel
How I Became a Werewolf — by Olive Alone
How to be a Witch — by Ruth Less
The Rich Man's Guide to Good Living — by Ivor Lot
Make Money from Rich Men — by Marie Mee

Novels

The Broken Window — by Eva Brick
The Short Break — by T.N. Cookies
Cry Baby — by Liza Weeping
The Monster Hanging off the Cliff — by Alf Hall
A Very Hungry Giant — by Ethan D. Lot

STATIONERY

Writing Paper

Why did the young witch have such difficulty
writing letters?
She had never learned to spell properly.

How does a ghost start a letter?
Tomb it may concern.

What do snakes write on the bottom of their
letters?
With love and hisses.

What did the werewolf write at the bottom of the
letter?
Best vicious . . .

What kind of letters did the snake get from his
admirers?
Fang mail.

Pens and Pencils

What do you get if you cross a tall green monster with a fountain pen?
The Ink-credible Hulk.

What does an executioner do with a pen and paper?
Writes his chopping list.

What do ghosts write with?
Phantom pens.

Vincent, why have you got a sausage stuck behind your ear?
Eh? Oh, no, I must have eaten my pencil for lunch!

Why is a pencil the heaviest thing in your bag?
Because it's full of lead.

Why did the man take a pencil to bed?
To draw the curtains . . . I'd tell you another joke
about a pencil, but it hasn't any point.

What do witches use pencil sharpeners for?
To keep their hats pointed.

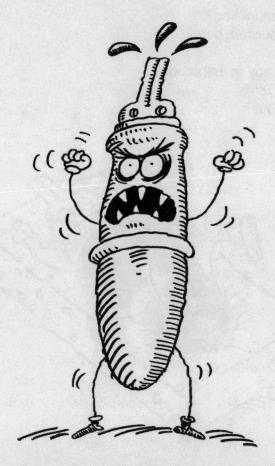

Ink

Mom, do you think the baby would like some blotting
paper to eat?
No, dear, I don't think he would. Why?
He's just swallowed a bottle of ink . . .

When is ink like a sheep?
When it's in a pen.

What is an inkling?
A baby fountain pen.

Have you any invisible ink?
Certainly, sir.
What colour?

GARDENING

Garden Furniture

Good news — two boys went out one day climbing trees.
Bad news — one of them fell out.
Good news — there was a hammock beneath him.
Bad news — there was a rake beside the hammock.
Good news — he missed the rake.
Bad news — he missed the hammock, too.

Garden Sheds

Dad, what are all the holes in the new garden shed?
They're knot-holes.
What do you mean they're not holes? I can put my finger into them.

Lawnmowers

What has four legs, a tail, whiskers and cuts grass?
A lawn miaower.

Lawn Care

Why is grass so dangerous?
Because it's full of blades.

What did the gardener say when he saw his non-too-bright assistant laying the lawn at a new house?
Green on top!

Flowers and Plants

Silly florist: I used to wear a flower in my lapel.
Customer: Why did you stop?
Florist: Because the pot kept hitting me in the stomach.

Did you hear about the florist who had two children?
One's a budding genius and the other's a blooming idiot.

What's a python's favorite flower?
Coily-flowers.

What is a frog's favorite flower?
The croakus.

What are the bees' favorite flowers?
Bee-gonias

What did the bee say to the flower?
Hello, honey.

Why did the bees go on strike?
Because they wanted more honey and shorter
working flowers.

Knock, knock.
Who's there?
Ivy.
Ivy who?
Ivy cast a spell on you.

What is a
witch with
poison ivy
called?
An itchy witchy.

There was a
young witch from
Nantes
Who hated each one
of her aunts
So she buried the
lot
In her vegetable
plot
And grew some
remarkable plants.

KNITTING AND SEWING

Knitting

How did the teacher knit a suit of armor?
She used steel wool.

Why did the monster knit herself three socks?
Because she grew another foot.

Ronald had broken a rib playing football. He went to the doctor, who asked how he was feeling. "I keep getting a stitch in my side," he replied.
"That's good," said the doctor. "It shows the bone is knitting."

Sewing

What's your handicrafts teacher like?
She's a sew and sew.

How do you poison a woman with a pair of scissors?
Give her arseanick!

Teacher: Spell the word "needle," Kenneth.
Kenneth: N-e-i-
Teacher: No, Kenneth, there's no "i" in needle.
Kenneth: Then it's a rotten needle, sir!

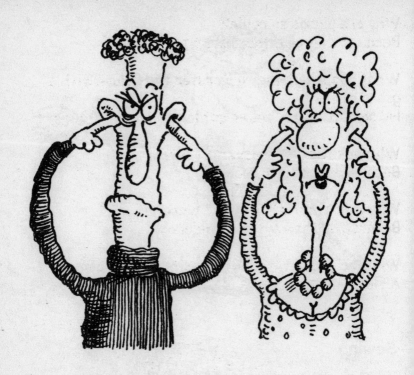

MUSICAL INSTRUMENTS

Pianos

Did you hear about the short-sighted monster who fell in love with a piano?
It had such wonderful white teeth, how could he resist it?

Piano Tuner: I've come to tune the piano.
Music Teacher: But we didn't send for you.
Piano Tuner: No, but the people who live across the street did.

Why are pianos so noble?
Because they're either upright or grand.

What happened when a monster fell in love with a grand piano?
He said, "Darling, you've got lovely teeth."

Why was the piano player arrested?
Because he got into treble.

Why is it difficult to open a piano?
Because all the keys are inside.

What do you get if King Kong sits on your piano?
A flat note.

Violins

A little monster was learning to play the violin. "I'm good, aren't I?" he asked his big brother.
"You should be on the radio," said the brother.
"You think I'm that good?"
"No, I think you're terrible, but at least if you were on the radio, I could switch you off."

What sort of violin does a ghost play?
A dreadivarius.

What were the Chicago gangster's last words?
Who put that violin in my violin case?

My brother's been practicing the violin for ten years.
Is he any good?
No. It was nine years before he found out he wasn't supposed to blow out.

112

Stephen, it's time for your violin lesson.
Oh, fiddle!

Guitars

Why did Silly Sue throw her guitar away?
Because it had a hole in the middle.

Sign on the school noticeboard: Guitar for sale,
cheap, no strings attached.

Trumpets and Trombones

With whom does an elastic trumpet player play?
With a rubber band.

Why did Ken keep his trumpet in the fridge?
Because he liked cool music.

What did the musical skeleton do?
Invented the trombone.

Drums and Percussion

Henry: I'd like to learn to play a drum, sir.
Music Teacher: Beat it!

What kind of musical instrument can you use for
fishing?
The cast-a-net.

SPORTS DEPARTMENT

Athletics

Hil: Who was the fastest runner in history?
Bill: Adam. He was first in the human race.

What creepie crawlies do athletes break?
Tapeworms.

Badminton

What is a vampire's favorite sport?
Batminton.

How does Dracula keep fit?
He plays batminton.

Ballet

"Ann," said the dance teacher. "There are two things stopping you becoming the world's greatest ballerina."
"What are they, ma'am?" asked Ann.
"Your feet."

What is a toad's favorite ballet?
Swamp Lake.

Baseball

Why do vampires like playing baseball?
Because they've got plenty of bats.

Boxing

If a boxer was knocked out by Dracula, what would he be?
Out for the Count.

Maeve: You remind me of my favorite boxer.
Dave: Mike Tyson?
Maeve: No, he's called Fido.

Which weight do ghosts box at?
Phantom weight.

Cricket

What animal is best at cricket?
A bat.

Croquet

Doctor, doctor, I think I'm turning into a frog.
Oh, you're just playing too much croquet.

Cycling

My dog is a nuisance. He chases everyone on a
bicycle. What can I do?
Take his bike away.

What is a ghost-proof bicycle?
One with no spooks in it.

"Lie flat on your backs, class, and circle your feet in the air as if you were riding your bikes," said the gym teacher. "Alec! What are you doing? Move your feet, boy."
"I'm freewheeling, sir."

Fishing

Two shark fishermen were sitting on the side of their boat just off the coast of Florida, cooling their feet in the sea. Suddenly an enormous shark swam up and bit off one fisherman's leg. "A shark's just bitten off my leg," yelled the fisherman.
"Which one?"
"I don't know. All sharks look the same to me."

Two fishermen were out in their boat one day when a hand appeared in the ocean. "What's that?" asked the first fisherman. "It looks as if someone's drowning!"
"Nonsense," said the second. "It was just a little wave."

Passer-by (to fisherman): Is this river any good for fish?
Fisherman: It must be. I can't get any of them to leave it.

Where do vampires go fishing?
In the blood stream.

A man was fishing in the jungle. After a while another angler came to join him. "Have you had any bites?" asked the second man.

"Yes, lots," replied the first one, "but they were all mosquitoes."

Football

Will: Why do you call that new player Cinderella?
Bill: Because he's always running away from the ball.

Bob had just missed a shot at goal, which meant the other team won. "I could kick myself," he groaned, as the players came off the pitch.

"Don't bother," said the captain, "you'd miss."

Captain: Why didn't you stop the ball?
Player: I thought that was what the net was for.

Did you hear about the idiotic goalkeeper who saved a penalty but let it in on the action replay?

Why is the ghouls' football pitch wet?
Because players keep dribbling on it.

George knocked on the door of his friend's house. When his friend's mother answered he said, "Can Albert come out to play?"
"No," said the mother, "it's too cold."
"Well, then," said George, "can his football come out to play?"

Why do centipedes make such poor football players?
By the time they put their boots on, the match is nearly over.

Golf

"What are the elements, Andrew?" asked the science teacher.
"Er . . . earth . . . air . . . fire . . ."
"Well done," said the teacher. "There's one more."
"Er . . . oh, yes. Golf."
"Golf!"
Yes, I heard my mother say that dad's in his element when he plays golf."

Riding

What do ghosts like about riding horses?
Ghoulloping.

Rollerblading

What's big, heavy, furry, dangerous and has sixteen wheels?
A monster on rollerblades.

Sailing

What happened to the boat that sank in the sea full of piranha fish?
It came back with a skeleton crew.

When is a boat like a fall of snow?
When it is a drift.

Skateboarding

What does a cannibal call a skateboarder?
Meals on wheels.

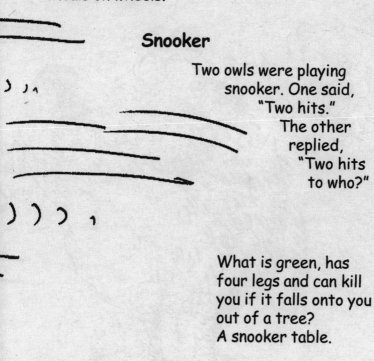

Snooker

Two owls were playing snooker. One said, "Two hits." The other replied, "Two hits to who?"

What is green, has four legs and can kill you if it falls onto you out of a tree?
A snooker table.

Did you hear about the snooker-mad monster? He went to the doctor because he didn't feel well.
"What do you eat?" asked the doctor.
"For breakfast I have a couple of red snooker balls, and at lunchtime I grab a black, a pink and two yellows. I have a brown with my tea in the afternoon, and then a blue and another pink for dinner."
"I know why you are not feeling well," exclaimed the doctor. "You're not getting enough greens."

Swimming

Why do you keep doing the backstroke?
I've just had lunch and don't want to swim on a full stomach.

Did you hear about the slow swimmer?
He could only do the crawl.

A man in a swimming pool was on the very top diving-board. He poised, lifted his arms, and was about to dive when the attendant came running up, shouting, "Don't dive — there's no water in that pool!"
"That's all right," said the man. "I can't swim!"

Jack: Dad, there's a man at the door collecting for a new swimming pool.
Father: Give him a bucket of water.

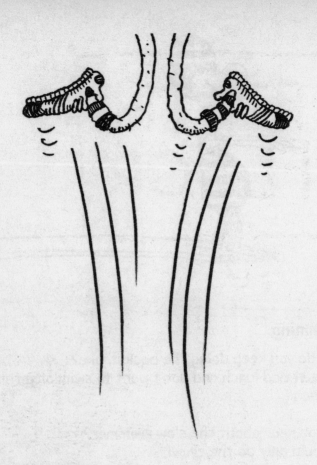

Trampolining

PE teacher: Well, Billy, how are you getting along with the trampolining?
Billy: Oh, up and down, you know.

PETS

What pet makes the loudest noise?
A trum-pet.

A woman walked into a pet shop and said, "I'd like a frog for my son."
"Sorry, ma'am," said the manager, "we don't do part exchange."

Did you hear about the man who took his pet skunk to the cinema?
During a break in the film, the woman sitting in front, who had been most affected by the animal's smell, turned round and said in a very sarcastic voice, "I'm surprised that an animal like that should appreciate a film like this."
"So am I," said the man. "He hated the book."

Witch: I'd like some tiles for my bathroom.
Salesman: But this is a pet shop.
Witch: That's all right — I want reptiles.

Parrots

A man went into a pet shop to buy a parrot. He was shown an especially fine one which he liked the look of, but he was puzzled by the two strings which were tied to its feet. "What are they for?" he asked the pet shop manager.

"Ah well, sir," came the reply, "that's a very unusual feature of this particular parrot. You see, he's a trained parrot, sir, he used to be in the circus. If you pull the string on his left foot he says 'Hello' and if you pull the string on his right foot he says 'Goodbye.'"

"And what happens if you pull both strings at once?"

"I fall off my perch, you fool!" screeched the parrot.

Why did a man's pet parrot not make a sound for five years?
It was stuffed.

My parrot lays square eggs.
That's amazing! Can it talk as well?
Yes, but only one word.
What's that?
Ouch!

How do you know you are haunted by a parrot?
He keeps saying "Ooo's a pretty boy then?"

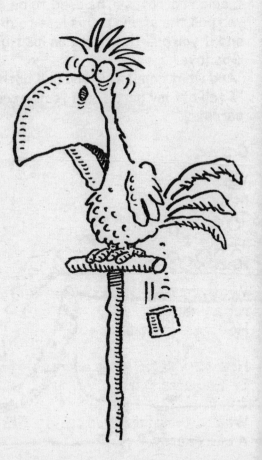

What do you get if you cross King Kong with a parrot?
A messy cage.

What do you get if you cross a centipede with a parrot?
A walkie-talkie.

Canary

What is large, yellow, lives in Scotland and has never been seen?
The Loch Ness Canary.

Rabbits

What do you get if you pour hot water down a rabbit hole?
Hot cross bunnies!

How can you tell when it's rabbit pie for dinner?
It has hares in it.

What do you get if you cross a flea with a rabbit?
A bug's bunny.

Hamsters

Little boy, in pet shop: I'd like to buy a hamster, please. How much do they cost?
Pet shop owner: £10 apiece.
Little boy, horrified: How much does a whole one cost?

Cats

What do you call a witch's cat that drinks vinegar?
A sour puss.

Why is a witch's kitten like an unhealed wound?
Both are a little pussy.

"Gosh, it's raining cats and dogs," said Suzie looking out of the window.
"I know," said her mother who had just come in.
"I've just stepped in a poodle!"

What's furry, has whiskers and chases outlaws?
A posse cat.

What's an American cat's favorite car?
A Catillac.

First cat: How did you get on in the milk-drinking contest?
Second cat: Oh, I won by six laps!

Witch: Doctor, doctor, I keep thinking I'm my own cat.
Doctor: How long have you thought this?
Witch: Since I was a kitten.

Why are cats such good singers?
They're very mewsical.

When it is unlucky to see a black cat?
When you're a mouse.

Why did the girl feed her cat with pennies?
She wanted to put them in the kitty.

What do you call a witch's cat who can do spells as well as her mistress?
An ex-purr-t.

There once was a very strong cat
Who had a big fight with a bat;
The bat flew away
At the end of the day,
And the cat had a scrap with a rat.

What does a cat go to sleep on?
A caterpillar.

First cat: Where do fleas go in winter?
Second cat: Search me!

What kind of cats love water?
Octopusses.

Dogs

Advertisement: Dog for sale. Really gentle. Eats anything. Especially fond of children.

What would you get if you crossed a frog with a little dog?
A croaker spaniel.

What fish do dogs chase?
Catfish.

My dog plays chess.
Your dog plays chess? He must be really clever!
Oh, I don't know. I usually beat him three times out of four.

Teacher: Who can tell me what "dogma" means?
Cheeky Charlie: It's a lady dog that's had puppies, sir.

What do you call a dog owned by Dracula?
A blood hound.

Would you like to play with our new dog?
He looks very fierce. Does he bite?
That's what I want to find out.

Mother: Keep that dog out of the house, it's full of fleas.
Son: Keep out of the house, Fido, it's full of fleas.

139

Why did the skeleton run up a tree?
Because a dog was after its bones.

Jim: Our dog is just like one of the family.
Fred: Which one?

What dog smells of onions?
A hot dog.

A man who bought a dog took it back, complaining
that it made a mess all over the house. "I thought
you said it was house-trained," he moaned.
"It is," said the previous owner. "It won't go
anywhere else."

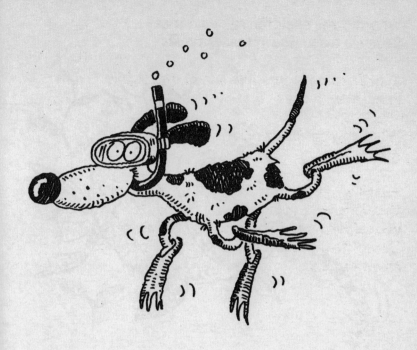

Fish

What did Dr Frankenstein get when he put his
goldfish's brain in the body of his dog?
I don't know, but it is great at chasing submarines.

What sort of fish performs surgical operations?
A sturgeon.

Doctor, doctor, my husband smells like a fish.
Poor sole!

One goldfish to his friend in the fish tank: "If
there's no God, who changes the water?"

Teacher: Martin, put some more water in the fish tank.
Martin: But, sir, they haven't drunk the water I gave them yesterday.

Snakes

A boa with coils uneven
Had the greatest trouble in breathing
With jokes she was afflicted
For her laughs got constricted
And her coils started writhing and wreathing.

Why are snakes hard to fool?
They have no leg to pull.

Stick insects

Why is the letter "t" so important to a stick insect?
Without it would be a sick insect.

What did one stick insect say to another?
Stick around.

sniff

TOYS

Only a week after Christmas an irate mom stormed into the toy shop. "I'm bringing back this unbreakable toy fire engine," she said to the man behind the counter. "It's useless!"
"Surely your son hasn't broken it already?" he asked.
"No, he's broken all his other toys with it."

Teddy Bears

What do baby witches play with?
Deady bears.

What do Paddington Bear and Winnie the Pooh pack for their holidays?
The bear essentials.

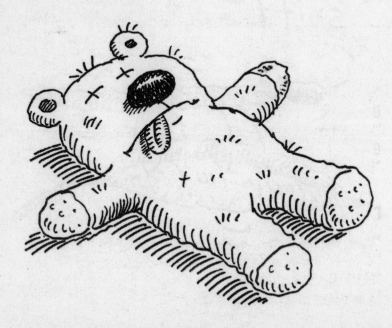

144

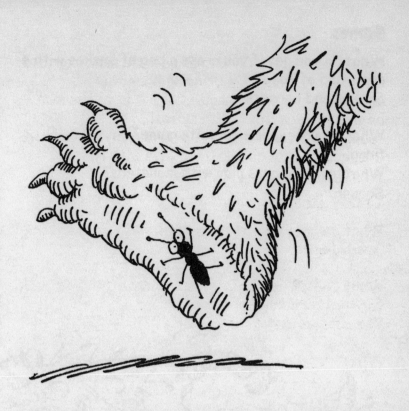

"Who's been eating my porridge?" squeaked Baby Bear.

"Who's been eating my porridge?" cried Mother Bear.

"Burp!" said Father Bear.

Dolls

"Why are you crying, Amanda?" asked her teacher.

"'Cos Jenny's broken my new doll," she cried.

"How did she do that?"

"I hit her on the head with it."

Games

What do you get if you cross a bag of snakes with a cupboard of food?
Snakes and Larders.

What's a crocodile's favorite game?
Snap!
What game do ants play with monsters?
Squash.

What is the favorite game at a ghost's Halloween party?
Hide and Shriek.

Doctor, doctor, I keep dreaming there are great, gooey, bug-eyed monsters playing tiddledywinks under my bed. What shall I do?
Hide the tiddledywinks.
Little brother: Look, Sis, I've got a pack of cards.
Big sister: Big deal!

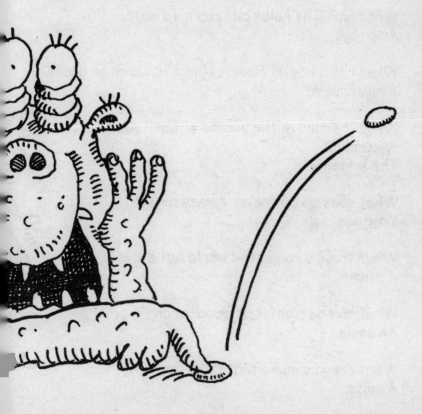

Puzzles and Riddles

What gets wetter the more it dries?
A towel.

What musical instrument never
tells the truth?
A lyre.

What knocks you out each night
but doesn't harm you?
Sleep.

What is full of holes but can hold water?
A sponge.

What room has no floor, ceiling, windows or doors?
A mushroom.

What is found in the middle of both America and
Australia?
The letter R.

What goes up but never comes down?
Your age.

What travels round the world but stays in a corner?
A stamp.

What can be right, but never wrong?
An angle.

What can you make that can't be seen?
A noise.

Magic Kits

What do you get if you cross a snake with a magician?
Abra da cobra.

What do you get if you cross a snake with a magic spell?
Addercadabra.

What would you get if you crossed a bat with a magician?
A flying sorcerer.

Why don't ghosts make good magicians.
You can see right through their tricks.

What did one magician say to another?
Who was that girl I sawed you with last night?

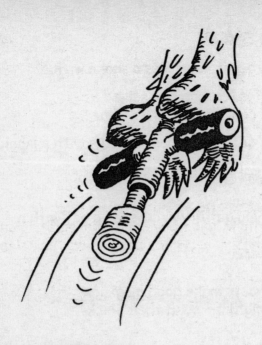

Paints and Crayons

What kind of ant can you color with?
A cray-ant.

Why did the monster paint himself in rainbow colors?
Because he wanted to hide in the crayon box.

Pogo Sticks

What is big, hairy and bounces up and down?
A monster on a pogo stick.

What happened when the skeletons rode pogo sticks?
They had a rattling good time.

SWEETIE SHOP

Chocolate

There once was a schoolboy named Rhett,
Who ate ten chocolate bars for a bet.
When asked "Are you faint?"
He said, "No, I ain't.
But I don't feel like flying a jet."

Johnny collected lots of money from trick-or-
treating and he went to buy some chocolate. "You
should give that money to charity," said the sales
girl.
Johnny thought for a moment and said, "No, I'll buy
the chocolate. You give the money to charity."

Come here, you greedy wretch. I'll teach you to eat all your sister's birthday chocolates!
It's all right, Dad, I know how.

Boy: What's black, slimy, with hairy legs and eyes on stalks?
Mom: Eat the chocolates and don't worry about what's in the box.

Jimmy, how many more times must I tell you to come away from that box of chocolates?
No more, mom. It's empty.

Sweeties

What happened when one jellyfish met another?
They produced jelly babies.

Two boys were walking through a churchyard one
dark and stormy night. As one stopped to do up his
shoelaces they heard an eerie voice coming from
behind one of the tombs saying, "Now that I've got
you, I'm going to eat your legs first, then your arms,
then you head and finally I'll gulp down your body."

Terrified, the boys ran for the exit but before
they could get out of the gate a figure in black
loomed before them. "I thought I heard someone,"
said the minister, "would you boys like a jelly baby?"

How do you get six monsters in a sweetie tin?
Take the sweeties out first.

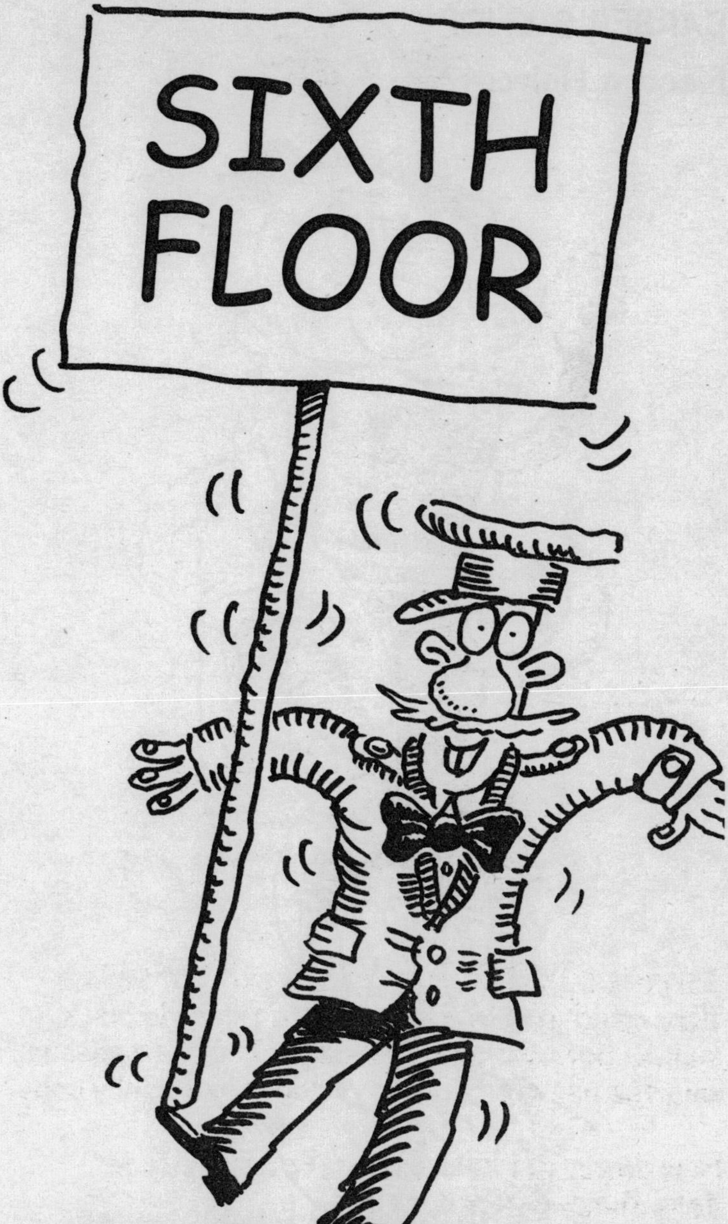
SIXTH
FLOOR

BARBER'S SHOP
Need a Haircut?

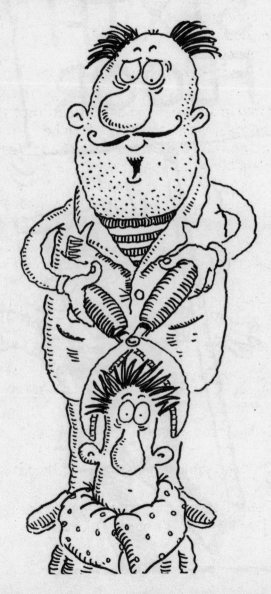

Why do barbers make good drivers?
Because they know all the short cuts.
Mean man: How much for a haircut?
Barber: Fifteen pounds.
Mean man: How much for a shave?
Barber: Ten pounds.
Mean man: Right — shave my head.

A man sitting in a barber's chair noticed that the barber's hands were very dirty. When he commented on this, the barber explained, "Yes, sir, no one's been in for a shampoo yet."

What do you part with, but never give away?
A comb.

Mommy, mommy, Sammy keeps saying I look like a werewolf.
Be quiet dear and go and comb your face.

Need a Shave?

What does Luke Skywalker shave with?
A laser blade.

Barber: Did you come in with a red scarf on?
Man: No.
Barber: Oh dear, I must have cut your throat.

Barber: Oops! Sorry, I've just cut your chin.
Vampire: Don't worry, it's not my blood.

What is grey and hairy and lives on a man's face?
A mousetache.

Hair Tonic

A wizard who's as bald as a bat
Spilt hair tonic over the mat
It's grown so much higher
He can't see the fire
And he thinks that it's smothered his cat.

HAIRDRESSERS AND BEAUTY SALON

Britain's oldest lady was 115 years old today, and
she hasn't got a grey hair on her head.
How come?
She's completely bald.

What do you get if you cross a hairdresser with a
werewolf?
A monster with an all-over perm.

Chris: Do you like my new hairstyle?
Fliss: In as much as it covers most of your face, yes.

How do warty witches keep their hair out of place?
With scare spray.

Need a Wig?

What kind of wig can hear?
An earwig.

Witch: Officer you must help. I've just lost my wig.
Police officer: Certainly, ma'am, we'll comb the area.

Beauty Salon

First witch: I spend hours in front of the mirror admiring my beauty. Do you think that's vanity?
Second witch: No, it's imagination.

Who won the Monster Beauty Contest?
No one.

First witch: I went to the beauty parlour yesterday. I was there for three hours.
Second witch: What did you have done?
First witch: Nothing, I was just going in for an estimate.

Peggy: I've just come back from the beauty parlour.
Piggy: Pity it was closed!

A witch went into a beauty parlour and asked the assistant how much it would cost to make her look like a film star.
"Nothing," replied the assistant.
"Nothing?" asked the witch, "But how can I look like a film star?"
"Haven't you seen a film called *The Creature from the Black Lagoon?*" replied the assistant.

First witch: My beauty is timeless.
Second witch: Yes, it could stop a clock.

A monster went to the doctor with a branch growing out of the top of his head. "Hmm," said the doctor. "I've no idea what it is." The next week the branch was covered in leaves and blossom. "I'm stumped, " said the doctor, "but you can try taking these pills." When the monster came back a month later, the branch had grown into a tree, and just a few weeks after that, it had developed into a small pond surrounded by trees and bushes. "Ah!" said the doctor, "I know what it is. You've got a beauty spot!"

DOCTOR'S SURGERY

A man rushed into the doctor's office, jumped on the doctor's back, and started screaming, "One! Two! Three! Four!"
"Wait a minute!" yelled the doctor, struggling to free himself. "What do you think you're doing?"
"Well, doctor," said the eccentric man, "they did say I could count on you!"

Doctor, doctor, there's an invisible ghost in the waiting room.
Tell him I can't see him without an appointment.

Doctor, doctor! Every time I drink a cup of tea I get a sharp pain in my nose.
Have you tried taking the spoon out of the cup?

Doctor, doctor, I feel like an apple!
We must get to the core of this.

163

Doctor, doctor, I think I'm a dog!
Sit down, please.
Oh no — I'm not allowed on the furniture.

Doctor, doctor, I keep thinking I'm a snake about to shed its skin.
Just slip into something more comfortable.

Doctor, doctor, I keep thinking I'm a moth.
So why did you come to see me?
Well, I saw the light in the window . . .

Doctor, doctor, I keep thinking I'm a python.
Oh, you can't get round me like that, you know.

Doctor, doctor, I feel like an insignificant worm.
Next!

Doctor, doctor, I keep thinking I'm the Abominable Snowman.
Just keep cool.

Doctor, doctor, I can't stand being so short any longer.
Then you'll just have to learn to be a little patient.

Doctor, doctor, I keep thinking I'm a bridge.
What on earth's come over you?
Six cars, two trucks and a bus.

Doctor, doctor, I keep thinking I'm a slice of bread.
Doctor: You've got to stop loafing around.

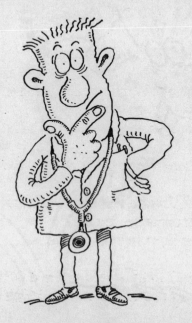

Doctor, doctor, I keep seeing a spinning insect.
Don't worry, it's just a bug that's going round.

Doctor, doctor, I'm becoming invisible!
Yes, I can see you're not all there.

Doctor, doctor, I've got a little sty.
Then you'd better buy a little pig.

Doctor, doctor, I keep thinking I'm a canary.
I can't tweet you, go and see a vet.

Witch: Doctor, doctor, I don't feel well.
Doctor: Don't worry, you'll just have to go to bed for a spell.

Doctor, doctor, can you give me something for my baldness?
How about a few pounds of pig manure?
Will that cure my baldness?
No, but with that on your head no one will come near enough to notice you're bald.

Doctor, doctor, I think I've been bitten by a vampire.
Drink this glass of water.
Will it make me better?
No, but I'll be able to see if your neck leaks.

Doctor: Good morning, Mrs Feather. Haven't seen you for a long time.
Mrs Feather: It's because I've been ill, doctor.

Skeleton: Doctor, doctor, I think I'm a yo-yo.
Doctor: Are you stringing me along?

Doctor: And did you drink your medicine after your bath, Mrs Soap?
Mrs Soap: No, doctor. By the time I'd drunk the bath there wasn't room for medicine.

Doctor: It's bad news, I'm afraid. You've only got five minutes to live.
Patient: But doctor, isn't there anything you can do for me?
Doctor, after some thought: Well, I could boil you an egg.

Cures

How do you cure a headache?
Put your head through a window, and the pane will disappear.

Sick Jokes

Why did the zombie go to hospital?
He wanted to learn a few sick jokes.

Why don't anteaters get sick?
Because they're full of anty-bodies!

What do you give a sick snake?
Asp-rin.

Did you hear about the sick ghost?
He had oooooo-ping cough.

Did you hear about the sick werewolf?
He lost his voice but it's howl right now.

OPTICIANS

A very shy young man went into an optician's one day to order a new pair of spectacles. Behind the counter was an extremely pretty young girl, which reduced the customer to total confusion. "Can I help you, sir?" she asked with a ravishing smile. "Er – yes – er – I want a pair of rim-speckled hornicles . . . I mean I want a pair of heck-rimmed spornicles . . . er . . . I mean . . ."
At which point the optician himself came to the rescue. "It's all right, Miss Jones. What the gentleman wants is a pair of rim-sporned hectacles."

A monster went to see the optician because he kept bumping into things. "You need glasses," said the optician.
"Will I be able to read with them?" asked the monster.
"Yes."
"That's brilliant," said the monster. "I didn't know how to read before."

Optician: You need spectacles.
Patient: How do you know?
Optician: I could tell as soon as you walked through the window.

171

Spectacles

"No, no, no!" said the enraged businessman to the persistent salesman. "I cannot see you today!"
"That's fine," said the salesman, "I'm selling spectacles."

Mr Timpson noticed his neighbor, Mr Simpson, searching very hard for something in his front yard.
"Have you lost something, Mr Simpson?" asked Mr Timpson.
"Yes," replied Mr Simpson. "I've mislaid my spectacles."
"Oh dear," said Mr Timpson.

"Where did you last see them?"
"In my sitting room," said Mr Simpson.
"In your sitting room?" asked Mr Timpson. "So why are you looking for them outside your house?"
"Oh," replied Mr Simpson, "there's more light out here!

Did you hear about the ghost who wore glasses?
They were spooktacles.

TRAVEL AGENCY

Getting Away

How do toads travel?
By hoppercraft.

What does a witch get if she's a poor traveler?
Broom sick.

They say he's going places.
The sooner the better!

What do you call a mosquito on vacation?
An itch-hiker.

A man telephoned London Airport.
How long does it take to get to New York?
Just a minute.
Thanks very much.

First witch: I'm going to France tomorrow.
Second witch: Are you going by broom?
First witch: No, by hoovercraft.

What British airline do vampires travel on?
British Scareways.

How do insects travel when they go on holiday?
They go for a buggy ride.

Passenger: Will this bus take me to New York?
Driver: Which part?
Passenger: All of me, of course!

What happened when a cannibal went on a self-
catering holiday?
He ate himself.

Why does Dracula always travel with his coffin?
Because his life is at stake.

Where do ghosts go for their holidays?
The Dead Sea.

Hotels

What did the teacher say after spending thousands in the expensive hotel?
I'm sorry to leave, now that I've almost bought the place.

Did you hear about the ghoul's favorite hotel?
It had running rot and mould in every room.

A new hotel porter was instructed by the manager that it was important to call the guests by their names, in order to make them feel welcome, and that the easiest way to find out their name was to look at their luggage. Armed with this advice, the porter took two guests up to their rooms, put down their bags and said, "I hope you have a very 'appy stay 'ere in Paris, Mr and Mrs Genuine Cowhide."

Ocean Cruises

Waiter on ocean liner: Would you like the menu, sir?
Monster: No, thank you. Just bring me the
passenger list.

City Breaks

Rome
How do we know that Rome was built at night?
Because all the books say it wasn't built in a day!

London

A boastful American from Texas was being shown the sights of London by a taxi driver. "What's that building there?" asked the Texan.

"That's the Tower of London, sir," replied the taxi driver.

"Say, we can put up buildings like that in two weeks," drawled the Texan. A little while later he said, "And what's that building we're passing now?"

"That's Buckingham Palace, sir, where the Queen lives."

"Is that so?" said the Texan. "Do you know back in Texas we could put a place like that up in a week?" A few minutes later they were passing Westminster Abbey. The American asked again, "Hey cabbie, what's that building over there?"

"I'm afraid I don't know, sir," replied the taxi driver. "It wasn't there this morning."

New York
Where does an American cow come from?
Moo York.

What's the smelliest city in America?
Phew York.

World Travel

North, Central and South America

Where do American ghosts go on holiday?
Lake Eerie.
Where is Dracula's American office?
The Vampire State Building.

What happened when two American stoats got married?
They became the United Stoats (States) of America.

Why are American schoolchildren extremely healthy?
Because they have a good constitution.

Did you hear about the Mexican who threw his wife over a cliff?
When the police officer asked him why he'd done it he said, "Tequila! Tequila!"

There was a little old lady from a small town in America who had to go to Texas. She was amazed at the size of her hotel and her suite. She went into the huge cafe and said to the waitress, who took her order for a cup of coffee, that she had never before seen anything as big as the hotel or her suite. "Everything's big in Texas ma'am," said the waitress. The coffee came in the biggest cup the old lady had ever seen. "I told you, ma'am, that everything is big in Texas," said the waitress. On her way back to her suite, the old lady got lost in the vast corridors. She opened the door of a darkened room and fell into an enormous swimming pool.

"Please!" she screamed. "Don't flush it!"

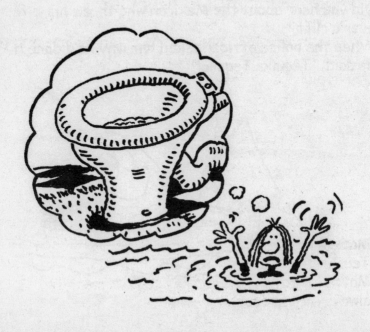

Boy: Where does the new kid come from?
Girl: Alaska.
Boy: Don't bother – I'll ask her myself.

Geography teacher: What is the coldest place in the world?
Ann: Chile.

Australia and New Zealand
What powerful reptile is found in Australia's Sydney Opera House?
The Lizard of Oz.

Teacher: Matthew, what is the climate of New Zealand?
Matthew: Very cold, sir.
Teacher: Wrong.
Matthew: But sir! When they send us meat, it always arrives frozen!

Europe

Tommy was saying his prayers as his father passed by his bedroom door. "God bless Mommy, and God bless Daddy, and please make Calais the capital of France."

"Tommy," said his father, "why do you want Calais to be the capital of France?"

"Because that's what I wrote in my geography test!"

Did you hear about the Frenchman who jumped into the river in Paris?
He was declared to be in Seine.

What makes Italy's Tower of Pisa lean?
It doesn't eat much.

A huge American car screeched to a halt in a sleepy
English village, and the driver called out to a local
inhabitant, "Say, am I on the right road for
Shakespeare's birthplace?"
"Ay, straight on, sir," said the rustic, "but no need
to hurry. He's dead."

An American tourist was visiting a quaint country
village in England, and got talking to an old man in
the local pub. "And have you lived here all your life,
Sir?" asked the American.
"Not yet, m'dear," said the villager wisely.

Adventure Holidays

First Explorer: There's one thing about Jenkinson.
Second Explorer: What's that?
First Explorer: He could go to headhunters' country
without any fear — they'd have no interest in him.

Why did the egg go into the jungle?
Because it was an eggsplorer.

SELF-SERVICE CAFE

Sign in a cafe: All drinking water in this establishment has been personally passed by the management.

Why was the cafe called "Out of this World"? Because it was full of Unidentified Frying Objects.

At our local cafe you can eat dirt cheap — but who wants to eat dirt?

Alex and Alan took their lunches to the local cafe to eat. "Hey!" shouted the proprietor. "You can't eat your own food in here!"
"OK," said Alex. So he and Alan swapped their sandwiches.

How did Frankenstein's monster eat his lunch?
He bolted it down.

What is a cannibal's favorite food?
Baked Beings.

What do you call a demon who slurps his food?
A goblin.

All-Day Breakfast Menu

This morning my dad gave me soap flakes instead of cornflakes for breakfast!
I bet you were mad.
Mad? I was foaming at the mouth!

What did the vampire say when he saw the neck of the sleeping man?
Ah! Breakfast in bed!

What do nasty monsters give each other for breakfast?
Smacks in the mouth.

What do cannibals eat for breakfast?
Buttered host.

Porridge and Cereal

Which ghost ate too much porridge?
Ghouldilocks.

What do you get if you cross a monster with a cow
and an oat field?
Lumpy porridge.

What is a termite's favorite breakfast?
Oak-meal.

What do witches' cats eat for breakfast?
Mice Krispies.

What do ghouls eat for breakfast?
Dreaded Wheat.

What noise does a witch's breakfast cereal make?
Snap, cackle, pop!

Two flies were on a cornflakes packet. "Why are we running so fast?" asked one.
"Because," said the second, "it says 'tear along the dotted line'!"

Honey and Jam
What did the spider say to the bee?
Your honey or your life.

Why do bees have sticky hair?
Because of the honey combs.

If bees make honey what do wasps make?
Waspberry jam.

What do traffic wardens like for tea?
Traffic jam sandwiches.

What happened to the demon who fell in the
marmalade jar?
Nothing, he was a jammy devil.

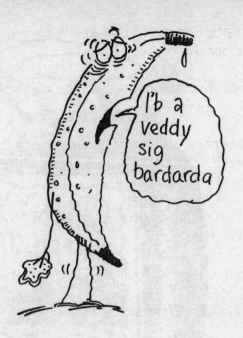

Fruit
Why are bananas never lonely?
Because they hang around in bunches.

What's the easiest way to make a banana split?
Cut it in half.

Why did the banana go out with the prune?
Because he couldn't find a date.

What's yellow and sniffs?
A banana with a bad cold.

They're not going to grow bananas any longer.
Really? Why not?
Because they're long enough already.

What's red and green and wears boxing gloves?
A fruit punch.

What did the grape do when the elephant sat on it?
It let out a little wine.

Why do grape harvesters have noses?
So they have something to pick during the growing season.

What is Dracula's favorite fruit?
Neck-tarines.

First apple: You look down in the dumps. What's eating you?
Second apple: Worms, I think.

What do you get if you cross an apple with a shellfish?
A crab apple.

Bacon and Eggs
What's the best day to eat bacon?
Fry-day.

Did you hear about the idiot farmer who made his chickens drink boiling water?
He thought they would lay hard-boiled eggs.

What do demons have for breakfast?
Deviled eggs.

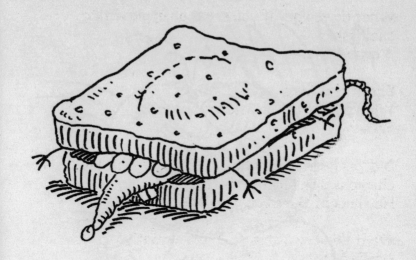

Lunch Menu

Sandwiches, Soups and Salads

What's grey and furry on the inside and white on the outside?
A mouse sandwich.

What cheese sandwich is made backwards?
Edam.

What did the baby ghost eat for dinner?
A boo-loney sandwich.

What do you call a witch who likes the beach but is scared of the water?
A chicken sand-witch.

What is a vampire's favorite soup?
Scream of tomato.

What sort of soup do skeletons like?
One with plenty of body in it.

Why did the tomato blush?
Because it saw the salad dressing.

Pasta
"My boyfriend says I look like a dishy Italian!" said
Miss Conceited.
"He's right," said her brother.
"Sophia Loren?"
"No – spaghetti!"

Did you hear about the Italian ghost?
He liked spooketti.

Burgers and Fries
Why did the teacher have her hair in a bun?
Because she had her nose in a hamburger.

What do you get if you cross a bee with a quarter
of a pound of ground beef?
A humburger.

What's white on the outside, green on the inside
and comes with relish and onions?
A hot frog.

Cakes, Cookies and Ice Cream

Why is history like a fruit cake?
Because it's full of dates.

What's the fastest cake in the world?
Meriiiiiiiiiiiiiiiinnnnnnnnnnnngue.

What cake wanted to rule the world?
Attila the Bun.

Knock, knock.
Who's there?
Woodworm.
Woodworm who?
Woodworm cake be enough or would you like two?

Did you hear about the man who stole some rhubarb?
He was put into custardy.

Why did the girl have to stop eating strawberry shortcake?
She was thick to her stomach.

What did the middle-aged man say as he tucked into his dessert?
I'm afraid all this food is going to waist.

What is a ghost's favorite dessert?
Boo-berry pie with I scream.

Why did the doughnut maker retire?
He was fed up with the hole business.

Why did Dracula have fang decay?
He was always eating fangcy cakes.

What is Dracula's favorite pudding?
Leeches and scream.

What do ghosts eat?
Dread and butter pudding.

What's the difference between a vampire and a cookie?
You can't dip a vampire in your tea.

Why did the cookie cry?
Because its mother had been a wafer too long.

Three cookies were crossing the road when the first one was knocked down. What did the third cookie say as he reached the pavement in safety? Crumbs!

Knock, knock.
Who's there?
Ice.
Ice who?
Ice cream, you scream, we all scream.

How do you make a vampire float?
        Take two scoops of ice-cream, a glass of Coke and add one vampire.

Drinks

Milk

What do ghosts like in their coffee?
Evaporated milk.

Mary had a bionic cow,
It lived on safety pins.
And every time she milked that cow.
The milk came out in tins.

What do we get from naughty cows?
Bad milk!

What do you get if you cross a cow and a camel?
Lumpy milkshakes!

Coffee, Tea and Cocoa
Where do vultures meet for coffee?
In a nest-cafe.

Knock, knock.
Who's there?
Larva.
Larva who?
Larva cup of coffee.

What do frogs drink?
Hot croako.

Lemonade and Cola
Jimmy: Is that lemonade OK?
Timmy: Yes. Why do you ask?
Jimmy: I just wondered if it was as sour as your face.

Why do vampires drink blood?
Lemonade makes them burp.

How do ghosts like their cola?
Ice ghoul.

What do frogs drink?
Croaka Cola.

RESTAURANT

A La Carte Dinner Menu
(with full waiter service)

At a restaurant which prided itself on its wide
selection of dishes, a customer was inspecting the
menu. "You'll find, sir," said the waiter proudly,
"that everything is on the menu. Absolutely
everything!"
"Yes, so I see," said the customer tartly, "so take it
back and bring me a clean one!"

Starters

Customer: Waiter, this soup tastes funny.
Waiter: So laugh, sir.

Waiter, waiter! There's a flea in my soup.
Tell him to hop it.

Waiter, waiter! There's a fly in my soup!
Don't worry, sir, the spider in your bread will get it.

Waiter, waiter! There are two flies in my soup.
That's all right, sir. Have the extra one on me.

Waiter, waiter! There's a fly in my soup.
Not fussy what they eat are they, sir?

Waiter, waiter, there's a fly in my soup.
Just a minute, sir, I'll get the fly spray.

Waiter, waiter! There's a spider in my soup. Send
for the manager!
It's no good, sir, he's frightened of them, too.

Waiter, waiter! There's a fly in my starter. Get rid
of it would you?
I can't do that, sir, he hasn't had his main course
yet.

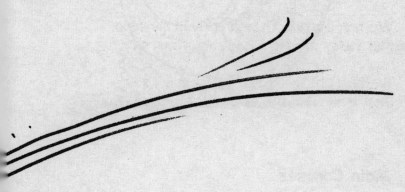

Waiter, waiter! What's this fly doing in my soup?
I think it's drowning, sir.

Waiter, waiter! What's this cockroach doing in my
soup?
We ran out of flies.

Main Courses

Meat and Fish
Waiter, this food isn't fit for a pig!
All right, I'll get you some that is.

Diner to Waiter: A pork chop, please and make it lean.
Waiter: Certainly, ma'am, which way?

Waiter, waiter, you have your thumb on my steak!
I know sir, I don't want it to fall on the floor again!

Waiter, waiter, could I have a mammoth steak please?
With pleasure, sir.
No, with ketchup, please.

Waiter: And how did you find your meat, sir?
Customer: Oh, I just lifted a potato and there it was.

There was a fight in the restauarant last night – a whole lot of fish got battered!

An irate customer in the restaurant complained that his fish was bad, so the waiter picked it up, smacked it and said, "Naughty, naughty, naughty!"

What is a sea monster's favorite dish?
Fish and ships.

Frogs' Legs and Snails

Waiter, waiter! Have you got frogs' legs?
No, sir, I always walk like this.

Waiter, waiter, do you have frogs' legs?
Yes sir.
Well then hop into the kitchen for my soup.

Waiter, waiter, can I have frogs' legs?
Well I suppose you could but you'd need surgery!

Waiter, waiter! Do you serve snails?
Sit down, sir, we'll serve anyone.

Salads and Vegetables
Waiter, waiter! There's a maggot in my salad.
Don't worry, he won't live long in that stuff.

Waiter, waiter! There's a slug in my salad.
I'm sorry, sir, I didn't know you were a vegetarian.

Waiter, waiter! There's a teeny beetle in my
broccoli.
I'll see if I can find a bigger one, ma'am.

Desserts and Coffee

Waiter, waiter! There's a fly in my custard.
I'll fetch him a spoon, sir.

Waiter, waiter, why is my apple pie all mashed up?
You did ask me to step on it, sir.

Waiter, waiter, this coffee tastes like mud.
I'm not surprised, sir, it was ground only a few
minutes ago.

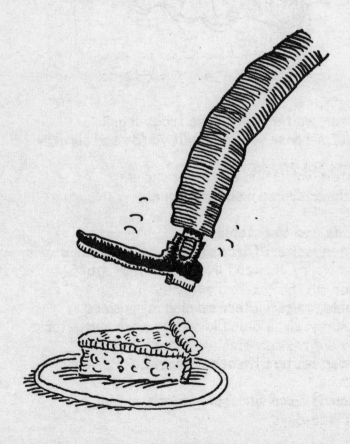

Cannibal Menu

First cannibal: Come and have dinner in our hut tonight.
Second cannibal: What are you having?
First cannibal: Hard-boiled legs.

What did the cannibal say when he was full?
I couldn't eat another mortal.

Why did the cannibal live on his own?
He was fed up with other people.

When do cannibals cook you?
On Fried-days.

What does a cannibal eat with cheese?
Pickled organs.

How can you help a starving cannibal?
Give him a helping hand.

What happens if you upset a cannibal?
You get into hot water.

How did the cannibal turn over a new leaf?
He became a vegetarian.

Two cannibals were having their dinner. One said to
the other, "I don't like your friend."
The other one said, "Well, put him to one side and
just eat the vegetables."

216

Table Manners

Did you hear about the mother who was trying to instil good table manners in her girls?
She told them that a well-brought-up girl never crumbles her bread or rolls in her soup.

What does a monster mother say to her kids at dinnertime?
Don't talk with someone in your mouth.

I smother my dinner with honey.
I've done it all my life.
It makes the food taste funny.
But the peas stay on my knife.

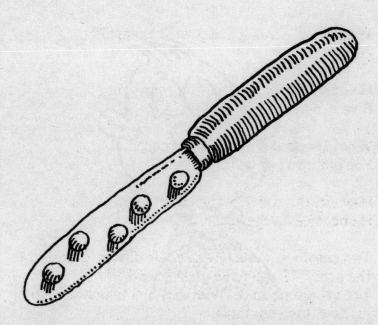

What did the monster want to eat in the monster restaurant?
The finger bowl.

Darren: I've just swallowed a bone.
Alexis: Are you choking?
Darren: No, I'm serious.

The food at the club dinner was awful. The soup tasted like dishwater, the fish was spoiled, the meat was overcooked, the vegetables were obviously old. The last straw for one member was the custard which was lumpy. "This meal is disgusting!" he roared. "And what's more, I'm going to bring it up at the annual meeting next week!"

SEASONAL

Christmas and New Year

What do you get if you cross a witch's cat with
Father Christmas?
Santa Claws.

Who carries a sack and bites people?
Santa Jaws.

What do witches sing at Christmas?
Deck the halls with poison ivy . . .

Here's your Christmas present. A box of your
favorite chocolates.
Wow, thanks! But they're half empty!
Well, they're my favorite chocolates, too!

220

What do Scully and Mulder look into in December?
The X-mas files.

What do angry rodents send each other at
Christmas?
Cross mouse cards.

What did the fireman's wife get for Christmas?
A ladder in her stocking.

What did the witch write in her Christmas card?
Best vicious of the season.

For our next Christmas dinner I'm going to cross a turkey with an octopus.
What on earth for?
So we can all have a leg each.

Alfie had been listening to his sister practice her singing. "Sis," he said, "I wish you'd sing Christmas carols."
"That's nice of you Alfie," she said, "why?"
"Then I'd only have to hear you once a year!"

What do vampires sing on New Year's Eve?
Auld Fang Syne.

Halloween

Why is the air so clean and healthy on Halloween?
Because so many witches are sweeping the sky.

How can you tell when witches are carrying a time
bomb?
You can hear their brooms tick!

A boy went to a Halloween party with a sheet over
his head. "Are you here as a ghost?" asked his
friends.
"No," he replied, "I'm an unmade bed."
Another boy wore a sheet over his head. "Are you an
unmade bed?" asked his friends.
"No, I'm an undercover agent," he replied.

What do witches eat at Halloween?
Spook-etti, Halloweenies, Devil's food cake and Boo-berry pie.

Witch: I've never been so insulted in my life! I went to a Halloween party, and at midnight they asked me to take my mask off.
Spook: Why are you so angry?
Witch: I wasn't wearing a mask.

Why did the wizard wear a yellow robe to the Halloween party?
He was going as a banana.

What happened to the girl who wore a mouse costume to her Halloween party?
The cat ate her.

What happened when the girl dressed as a spoon left the Halloween party?
No one moved. They couldn't stir without her.

Where do ghoulies go to on the day before Halloween party?
To the boo-ty parlour.

Who did the ghost invite to his party?
Anyone he could dig up.

What happened to the ghost who went to a party?
He had a wail of a time.

What happened when a ghost asked for a brandy at a party?
The waiter said "Sorry, we don't serve spirits."

Why didn't the skeleton go to the party?
He had no body to go with.

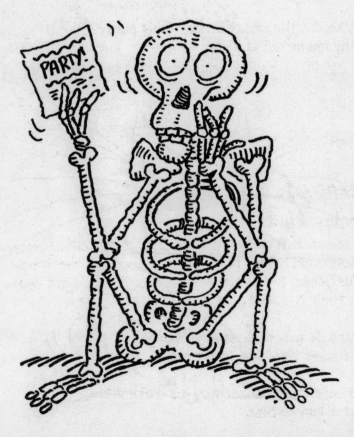

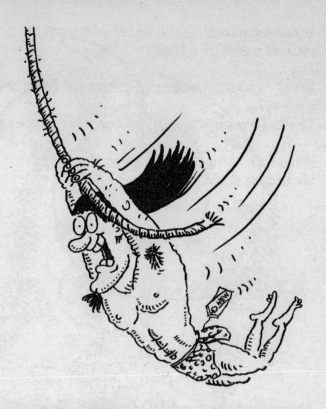

BARGAIN BASEMENT

Sales Goods

Trader: Roll up, roll up! Come to our mammoth sale.
Mammoth bargains to be had in our mammoth sale.
Customer: Forget it! No one round here's got room
in their houses for a mammoth.

Why do witches get good bargains?
Because they like to haggle.

Where does Tarzan buy his clothes?
At a Jungle Sale.

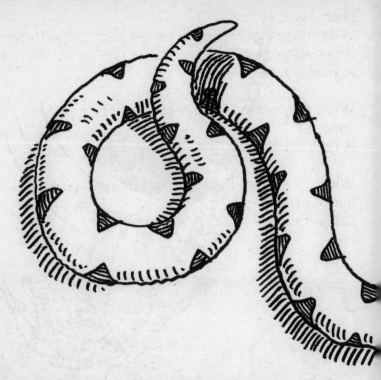

Miscellaneous and Damaged Goods

What do you get if you cross a yeti with a kangaroo?
A fur coat with big pockets.

What do you get if you cross a witch's cat and a canary?
A cat with a full tummy.

What do you get if you cross a snake with a pig?
A boar constrictor.

What do you get if you cross the Loch Ness Monster with a shark?

Loch Jaws.
What do you get if you cross an elephant with the
Abominable Snowman?
A jumbo yeti.

What do you get if you cross a vampire with Al
Capone?
A fangster!

What do you get if you cross a sheep-dog and a
bunch of daisies?
Collie-flowers!

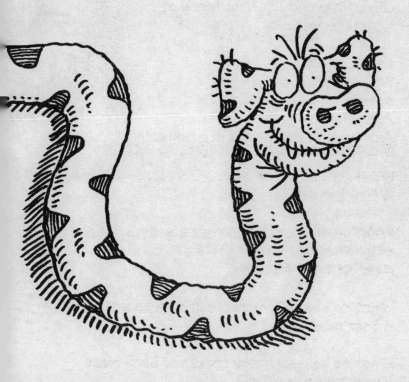

Monster Bargains

Knock, knock.
Who's there?
Turner.
Turner who?
Turner round, there's a monster
breathing down your neck.

Knock, knock.
Who's there?
Oliver.
Oliver who?
Oliver lone and I'm frightened of
monsters.

Knock, knock.
Who's there?
Aida.
Aida who?
Aida whole village 'cos I'm a monster.

Knock, knock.
Who's there?
Teheran.
Teheran who?
Teheran very slowly — there's a
monster behind you.

What did the monster say when he saw a rush-hour train full of passengers?
Oh good! A chew-chew train!

Howlers (and Things That Go Bump in the Basement)

Did you hear about the comedian who entertained at a werewolves' party?
He had them howling in the aisles.

Did you hear about the sick werewolf?
He lost his voice but it's howl right now.

What happened to the werewolf who ate garlic?
His bark was worse than his bite.

What do you call a ghost who only haunts the Town Hall?
The nightmayor.

Why did the ghost go trick-or-treating on the top floor?
He was in high spirits.

Woman in bed: Aaagh! Aaagh! A ghost just floated into my room!
Ghost: Don't worry, ma'am, I'm just passing through.

What did one ghost say to another?
I'm sorry, but I just don't believe in people.

What do you call a ghost who's always sleeping?
Lazy bones.

What kind of ghoul has the best hearing?
The eeriest.

What kind of street does a ghost like best?
A dead end.

What did the papa ghost say to the baby ghost?
Fasten your sheet belt.

What do you call a ghost that stays out all night?
A fresh air freak.

Why did the ghost go to the funfair.
He wanted to go on the rollerghoster.

Why did the ghost work at Scotland Yard?
He was the Chief In-Spectre.

What is a ghost boxer called?
A phantomweight.

Did you hear about the ghost comedian?
He was booed off stage.

Did you hear about the ghost who learnt to fly?
He was pleased to be back on terror-firma.

What are pupils at ghost schools called?
Ghoulboys and ghoulgirls.

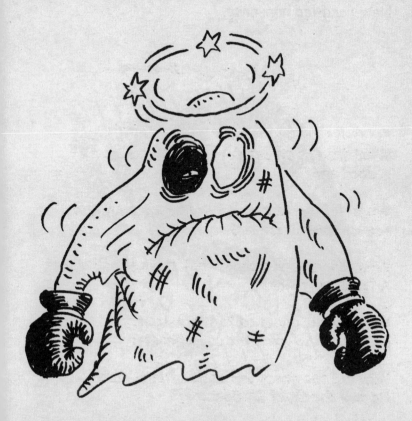

What do you get if you cross a ghost with a packet of potato chips?
Snacks that go crunch in the night.

A man was staying in a big old house and in the middle of the night he met a ghost. The ghost said, "I have been walking these corridors for 300 years."
The man said, "In that case, can you tell me the way to the toilet?"

What do vampires think of blood transfusions?
New-fang-led nonsense.

Why are vampire families so close?
Because blood is thicker than water.

What's Dracula's car called?
A mobile blood unit.

What do you get if you cross a midget with Dracula?
A vampire that sucks blood from your kneecaps.

Bargain Bug and Bat Jokes
(Buy One Get Ten Free)

What do you get if you cross an ant with one leg of an overall?
Pant.

What do you call an ant that likes to be alone?
An independ-ant.

What do you call an ant with frog's legs?
An ant-phibian.

What do you call an eighty-year-old ant?
An antique.

What's the biggest ant in the world?
An eleph-ant.
What is even bigger than that?
A gi-ant.

What do you call an ant who lives with your great-uncle?
Your great-ant.

What is smaller than an ant's dinner?
An ant's mouth.

How many ants are needed to fill an apartment?
Ten-ants.

Where do ants eat?
In a restaur-ant.

What do you call a smart ant?
Eleg-ant.

What kind of ants are very learned?
Ped-ants.

What do you call a foreign ant?
Import-ant.

Where do ants go for their holidays?
Fr-ants.

What do you call a greedy ant?
An anteater.

What do you call a scruffy, lazy ant?
Decad-ant.

What do you get if you cross some ants with some tics?
All sorts of antics.

What do you call an ant who honestly hates school?
A tru-ant.

What do you call an amorous insect?
The Love Bug.

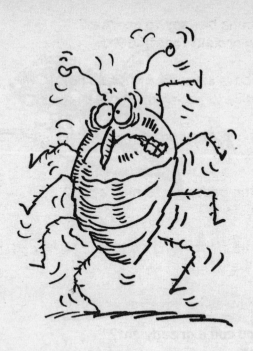

Which fly makes films?
Stephen Spielbug.

What do you call a nervous insect?
Jitterbug.

What do you call an insect from outer space?
Bug Rogers.

What kind of bee hums and drops things?
A fumble bee.

What did the confused bee say?
To bee or not to bee.

What did one bat say to another?
Let's hang around together.

What do bats sing when it's raining?
Raindrops keep falling on my feet.

What did a mommy bat say to her naughty son?
You bat boy.

What is the best way to hold a bat?
By its handle.

What is the first thing that bats learn at school?
The alphabat.

What do you call a bat in a belfry?
A dingbat.

ding

Cut Price and End of Line

So why did you keep turning people into Mickey
Mouse?
I was having Disney spells.

Have you heard the joke about the wall?
You'd never get over it.

Why do witches only ride their broomsticks after
dark?
That's the time to go to sweep.

What did the shy pebble monster say?
I wish I was a little boulder.

What did the dragon say when he saw Saint George
in his shining armor?
Oh no, not more tinned food!

What do you call an alien starship that drips water?
A crying saucer.

Little Miss Muffet
Sat on a tuffet
Eating a bowl of stew
Along came a spider
And sat down beside her.
Guess what? She ate him up too!

What is the definition of a narrow squeak?
A thin mouse.

Smarties Books are:
Fun, colourful, interactive, imaginative, creative, wacky and there's lots in them.

Other books available

Smarties Smart Art ☐
For creative geniuses everywhere, especially on rainy days.
ISBN: 1 84119 155 8
Price: £2.99

Smarties Puzzle Busters ☐
Can you help the puzzle busters crack exciting crimes and weird mysteries?
ISBN: 1 84119 154 X
Price: £2.99

Smarties Travel Teasers ☐
Ridiculous riddles, teasers, games and puzzles for all those boring journeys.
ISBN: 1 84119 153 1
Price: £2.99

Smarties Chuckle Factory ☐
How to giggle your way through boring bits of the holidays.
ISBN: 1 84119 156 6
Price: £2.99

Robinson books are available from all good bookshops
or direct from the publishers.
Just tick the titles you want and fill in the form overleaf.

TBS Direct
Colchester Road, Frating Green, Colchester, Essex CO7 7DW
Tel: +44 (0) 1206 255777
Fax: +44 (0) 1206 255914 Email: sales@tbs-ltd.co.uk

UK/BFPO customers please allow £1.00 for p&p for the first book,
plus 30p for each additional book up to a maximum charge of £3.00.
Please send me the titles ticked.
Overseas customers (inc. Ireland). please allow £2.00 for the first
book, plus £1.00 for the second, plus 50p for each additional book.

NAME (Block letters) ....

ADDRESS ....

....

POSTCODE ....

I enclose a cheque/PO (payable to TBS Direct) for ....

I wish to pay by Switch/Credit card ....

Number ....

Card Expiry Date ....

Switch Issue Number ....